Of Human Kindness

Of Human Kindness

What Shakespeare Teaches Us About Empathy

PAULA MARANTZ COHEN

Yale UNIVERSITY PRESS

New Haven and London

Yale University Press books may be purchased in quantity for educational, business, or promotional use. For information, please e-mail sales.press@yale.edu (U.S. office) or sales@yaleup.co.uk (U.K. office).

Set in Minion type by IDS Infotech, Ltd.
Printed in the United States of America.

Library of Congress Control Number: 2020940167
ISBN 978-0-300-25641-3 (hardcover : alk. paper)

A catalogue record for this book is available from the British Library.

This paper meets the requirements of ANSI/NISO Z39.48–1992 (Permanence of Paper).

10 9 8 7 6 5 4 3 2 1

For my students

Contents

Preface

The idea for this book grew out of my many years teaching Shakespeare to undergraduates. Most of these students had had limited exposure to Shakespeare and approached the reading without the veneer of knowingness that can stunt new insight. Their open, unbiased response helped me see the plays freshly and discern the pattern of developing empathy that I have come to understand as an important facet of Shakespeare's genius.

I began to chronicle my teaching experience in "Class Notes," a series of columns in the *American Scholar,* and in several op-ed pieces for the *Wall Street Journal.* When these appeared, I was surprised by the many online comments, personal emails, and handwritten letters that I received from readers. Two essays in particular—on Shylock as villain and victim in *The Merchant of Venice,* and on *King Lear* and aging—provoked a deluge of responses and convinced me to write this book. I hope that my discussion of how Shakespeare's greatest characters were built on a *learned* sense of empathy will be as illuminating and useful for others as it has been for me and my students.

All citations and spellings from the plays are from *The Bedford Shakespeare*, based on *The New Cambridge Shakespeare Edition*, ed. Russ McDonald and Lena Cowen Orlin (Boston: Bedford/ St. Martin's, 2015).

Of Human Kindness

Introduction

I spent my teenage years stretched out on the living room couch reading novels—Victorian triple-deckers with earnest, morally uplifting plots and characters. I could lose myself in these books and make believe that I was one of their virtuous, long-suffering heroines, destined to find my high-minded soul mate at the end. This made me feel secretly vindicated as a superior person and less like the odd and awkward adolescent I was.

I went on to study nineteenth-century literature in college and graduate school, and to teach this literature at a university. It continued to be reassuring for me and for my students to feel we were like the exceptional heroes and heroines in these books and not like the "ordinary" people who surrounded us. Quite frankly, I was a snob, and I encouraged snobbism in my classroom.

Until I began to teach Shakespeare.

This happened twenty years ago, when the Shakespeare expert at my university retired and I stepped in to replace her. Although I had read the major plays in college and seen numerous live and film productions, I had never studied Shakespeare's canon closely. But I was a seasoned teacher by this point, and

I knew that *not* being an expert can have its advantages. It can allow for more openness to others' viewpoints and more originality in one's own. I also suspected that I might learn something—that my diet of nineteenth-century literature needed to be supplemented by wider and more generous nourishment.

Teaching Shakespeare on a regular basis, I came to appreciate his greatness in a new way. This is not to refute the familiar pronouncements: that Shakespeare is a master of the English language and a superb poet; that his plays contain complex and varied characters; that they are full of clever wordplay, exceptional wit, and laugh-out-loud farce; and that they can be productively parsed using the latest literary and cultural theory. But I came to understand something more—namely, the way Shakespeare's characters made me *feel*, and how feeling that way made me a better person.

I should note that I began teaching Shakespeare at a time when his place in the university was being questioned. He was the product of an entrenched patriarchal society in which women were not allowed to perform onstage. His audience was almost entirely white and Christian. What relevance did he have in a multicultural classroom?

This question was not a theoretical one. My university had undergone a transformation since I began teaching there in 1982. It had evolved from a predominantly male engineering- and business-focused school into a comprehensive institution in which there were now as many women as men. These students were of varied ethnicity, religious affiliation, economic background, and gender identification; my class list reflected the diversity not only of our nation but of our world. Yet Shakespeare's plays, written more than four hundred years ago in a closed, homogenous society, spoke to these students in a way that no other work I have ever taught has been able to do.

The insights and range of identification my students derived from the plays astonished me—and continues to do so today, more than twenty years later.

The late eminent and erratically brilliant literary critic Harold Bloom asserted that Shakespeare "invented the human"—a reference to the rich interior lives of his characters.[1] What I want to argue here, and what my experience teaching the plays has demonstrated, is that this human dimension also involves an intimate connection to *us*, who study him. Shakespeare invented complex individuals who elicit *empathy*, whom we, audience or readers, feel for even when they fall outside the realm of our own experience.

When we think of the emotional effect of great drama, we think of *catharsis*, the term used by Aristotle to denote the outpouring of emotion—of pity and fear—that an audience is supposed to feel at the end of a tragedy. Watching characters brought low by fate and their own shortcomings is supposed to purge us of repressed emotion—to cleanse us of the anxiety and sadness that weigh us down. But emotional release of this kind can be isolating and self-indulgent, a way of avoiding responsibility for others' suffering. It can make us more complacent about who we are, more able to function smoothly and efficiently in the world as it exists. *Empathetic* emotion, by contrast, is disruptive. It is a humanizing and potentially instrumental variation on catharsis.

Empathy involves feeling beyond the self—feeling for others—and, at its most extreme, feeling for *the Other:* the individual whom we are superficially unable to identify with and feel for.[2] This is the case, most notably, for Shylock in *The Merchant of Venice,* who prepares the way, as I shall argue, for Othello and Lear—monumental, tragic figures who are ostensibly nothing like us yet are capable of making us see, understand,

and feel for them in their difference. Shakespeare's ability to create such characters, comprehensible even when they are unsympathetic and entirely alien to our experience, is reflective of his particular genius.

But what makes my argument so useful is the realization that Shakespeare's ability to feel and evoke empathy did not come into being fully formed. He *learned* empathy for a wide range of human beings not only by living a life that brought him into contact with diverse people but also through the process of writing his plays. Shakespeare grew both more empathetic and better at relaying empathy *as* he wrote, using the hints of earlier characters to flesh out later ones. I say this because I understand how the act of writing can create new insight and inspire growth. I also say this because, having spent so much time reading and teaching Shakespeare's work, I have been able to trace the development of his characters—to see how they build on one another in eliciting empathy.

My reading of Shakespeare has affected my own development as well. It has made me a better wife, mother, and teacher. When I took on an administrative role at my university six years ago—a position that I never thought I had the temperament to do—I found that the lessons I learned from Shakespeare served me here, too. The Victorian literature that was my first love and in which I was trained as a scholar had been far more doctrinaire and singular in its sense of what was true and virtuous. Shakespeare expanded my horizons, complicated my thinking, and, by extension, deepened my humanity.

I write this now in the belief that others can profit from the lessons I learned. We are living in a time when empathy seems in short supply—when our nation and our world are riven by polarities and misunderstandings. If we can learn to pause and think about where others are coming from, we may begin to heal the wounds in our communities and make more endurable the pain that we all face as mortal beings. For the *Other* exists within us as well as outside us. This is a lesson that Shakespeare teaches as well: how to recognize our own divided nature and embrace the human condition in which we all share.

1

Shakespeare's Empathetic Imagination

What was the method Shakespeare followed in the development of an empathetic imagination? How did he travel from an adolescent, lovesick Romeo to a mature, passion-driven Antony; from a flat if delightfully conniving Richard III to a profoundly divided Hamlet and an abused, murderously jealous Othello—characters who challenge us to feel more deeply beyond ourselves? One might argue that time and practice made Shakespeare wiser and more adept, but this seems to me to beg the question. There must have been a foundation, some kind of scaffold, on which time and practice anchored and elaborated themselves.

That scaffold, I contend, was "the Great Chain of Being," the cosmic moral hierarchy that the Elizabethans inherited from medieval Christian theology.[1] God stood at the top of the chain embodying absolute order; Satan at the bottom, embodying absolute disorder or chaos. This fundamental dualism was an

organizing principle of the Elizabethan worldview: God and
Satan and their various lesser representatives were in continual battle for control in the world and for the human soul, which,
in modern terms, we would call our character. For Shakespeare,
this Manichaean battle was a starting point for the elaboration
of his plots. It would drive him both to develop and to deviate
from an original template. It would cause him to acquire
greater empathy for different kinds of people—and to elicit
empathy in those attentive to what he wrote.

Shakespeare's use of contrasting, often warring structures,
inherited from his culture's theological worldview, was, in short,
more than a simple tool for composition or the creation of
dramatic conflict. It was a means of inspiring habits of mind in
the playwright, with the result that greater attention begins to
center on the figure who stands in opposition to the society's
norms.[2] Shakespeare may have begun with a conventional sense
of how a hero or, indeed, a person worthy of notice acted. But
by placing such a person in dramatic opposition to another who
was different and who generated the difficulty and the interest
of the plot, he was compelled, given the nature of his genius, to
imagine what that Other was like: to produce dialogue and
performed inner thoughts (soliloquies) for that character and
thereby imbue the character with complex human dimensions.
This imaginative transformation did not happen in a vacuum.
We know very little about Shakespeare's life, but we can specu-
late that experiences in his upbringing and career, nourished
by his unusually observant and sensitive nature, made him
susceptible to the habit of empathetic imagination.[3]

This habit would, over time, produce more and more original
effects—original insofar as they would involve finding interest and
meaning in characters who in other hands would have been flat
antagonists: villains or simple foils for the hero. Eventually,
we see such figures taking centerstage—if not becoming heroes

themselves, certainly becoming more comprehensible, even admirable in their Otherness—and forcing us to see aspects of ourselves, otherwise unacknowledged or hidden, in them. This process begins through contrast; the antagonist to the hero becomes a locus of interest rather than a simple foil. We have only to measure the distance between Richard III, an engagingly tricky but essentially one-dimensional villain with no clear antagonist, and the more complex character of Richard II, who grows in dimension as he faces Bullingbrook, the future Henry IV. The process is elaborated when we arrive at Henry's son Hal, later Henry V, whose personality has been further complicated through his positioning with respect to a range of other characters. As we progress through the canon, we see the playwright develop characters who, at an earlier point in his career, might not have figured in the action or might have been left in undeveloped, stereotypical form.

All writers tend to repeat themselves, to retrace patterning used before, and to indulge in compositional habits that make it easier to get from here to there. I know this from my own experience as a fiction writer who returns to certain structures of plot and character for reasons of laziness or convenience. In Shakespeare, however, this repetitive patterning seems to have been more than a compositional crutch. Far from promoting laziness, it was a spur to conceptual amplification and the rethinking of established ideas. His imagination was not conventionally fertile (most of his plots were borrowed from other sources), but it was elaborative and richly analogical. Once he imagined more about a given kind of character, he could not go back, and, indeed, was driven to extend that imagining to other kinds of characters, similarly placed.

Since I have tried to look at empathy in Shakespeare's plays as a function of his development as a playwright, some of my assumptions about chronology might be challenged. Speculation about dating varies for the histories and early comedies, in particular. It would seem to me, however, that Shakespeare was driven to work quickly and have a number of plays ready for performance at the same time, so one work might well have influenced another, even if it was technically completed later.

Despite uncertainty regarding chronology, the principal evolutionary arc in Shakespeare's canon seems to me irrefutable: the British histories and early comedies lead into the great tragedies—*Hamlet, Othello,* and *Lear,* in particular—which are especially attuned to Otherness as it exists both in the society and in the self. The plays that have been labeled Romances, which assimilate tragic elements to a philosophical long view in which things end happily, complete the canon.

And yet it is in one earlier work that I see the playwright's most important breakthrough with regard to empathy. *The Merchant of Venice,* written before the great tragedies, seems to have found its way to a rounded representation of the Jew Shylock almost by default—as if Shakespeare were forced in this direction by virtue of the twists and turns of the plot he borrowed from his sources. No work that I know of is such a dramatic example of form dictating content or, as the communication theorist Marshall McLuhan would say, of the medium shaping the message.[4] This play is further complicated by its representation of a suggestively homosexual character, at once poignant and responsible for setting in motion the maliciousness that permeates the action, and of a female character who doles out the eventual justice with an ample dose of cruelty. These characters will return in altered form in Shakespeare's subsequent plays. As I shall argue, there could not have been an Othello if there had not been a Shylock before him.

I am writing this book at a time when Shakespeare is no longer at the center of the university curriculum. Colleges no longer place as much stress on the humanities as they once did, but even in the context of literary study, Shakespeare has lost ground. He has been displaced by authors supposedly more relevant and enlightened. And yet I still see students who say they love Shakespeare, though their contact with him has been rudimentary or slight. Some of this passion is put on: Shakespeare is hard, at least when encountered for the first time, and for certain people there is glamour in what is hard. But these students' response, I am convinced, is more often genuine. They have been moved by the power of the plays, by an enduring charisma that makes itself felt even when the work is poorly taught or barely understood. What concerns me is that this exposure is diminishing and that fewer students are given the chance to read Shakespeare in high school and college. His absence in these formative educational contexts is bound to be a profound loss to humanity.

There is no denying that Shakespeare was the product of another time and, as a result, implicated in the sins of that time—that is, the patriarchal, colonialist, misogynist, and racist aspects of his society and culture. Yet his ability to understand the inequities and injustices of his world and to trace their effects on human character and relationships was exceptional. I know of no other author who has Shakespeare's penetrating consciousness of how we shape and are shaped by the society we live in.

My claims in this book derive from my having read Shakespeare closely with the help of two decades of undergraduate students whose insights extended and deepened my own. I deliberately refer to *reading*, knowing that this focus runs counter to the fact that Shakespeare was, first and foremost, a playwright. Didn't he write his plays to be performed? Wasn't he himself an actor who acutely understood the dynamics of the stage? He did and he was. But he was also a great poet and thinker whose full profundity can be grasped only through a close reading of what he put on the page. A great performance is a singular interpretation; it filters the play through the lens of the director. The language in performance also goes by quickly, and even if spoken by the best actors, a great deal of what exists in the text is necessarily lost. This problem extends to the classroom. Even with the words in front of them, professors can be as single-minded as directors in their interpretation of the plays, and students are often rushed when they read—hence their too-frequent resort to summaries and "translations" of Shakespeare's language. This problem is compounded when secondary material such as theory and criticism is added to the requirements for the course. But these are obstacles worth combating. Close reading is the best way to fully appreciate Shakespeare's genius. I wrote this book to elucidate and justify that method.

There are many insights to be derived from Shakespeare. But the one that I hope to relay here has to do with his ability to learn and teach empathy. Empathy is not simply a matter of imagining what "I" would feel in another's position. It is imagining what someone else feels who is not me—someone with a background, situation, and body different from my own. This is the challenge that reading Shakespeare addresses in a way not available as profoundly or efficiently through any other means. The depth and range with which he was able to imagine Otherness in his characters, and the degree to which that imagining remains valid, are, I maintain, unparalleled. His plays present the case for the Other without idealizing victimhood or forgetting the degree to which we all participate in the tragedy of the human condition: that we are all sentenced to death and ought to be humbled and compassionate in this awareness.

An ever-broadening empathy is what Shakespeare developed through the process of writing his plays, and it is what we can develop if we carry his insights into the creative work of our lives.

2

Richard III

Unrealized Potential

S hakespeare began his playwrighting career with eight
history plays written between 1589 and 1599. These
plays, which have collectively been called the Henriad
(since three kings named Henry figure in them), focus
on a continuous stretch of British history, though they are
viewed as two groups of four plays, or tetralogies, because they
were written in two discrete periods.

The Henriad taken as a whole depicts a time span that
preceded the ascendance to the throne of Shakespeare's then-
monarch, Queen Elizabeth I. The plays explore the drama of
Elizabeth's ancestry, culminating in what has been termed the
Tudor Myth: the idea that Elizabeth's grandfather Henry VII,
by uniting the previously warring houses of Lancaster and York,
ushered in an unparalleled era of prosperity and peace.

Shakespeare knew the value of dramatizing this flattering
narrative. He was an astute promoter and businessman as well
as a playwright, poet, and actor. He was always aware of the

audience range for his plays, from the lower-class "groundlings" who paid a nominal sum to stand during productions to the gentry and nobility who occupied the expensive seats. Ultimately, he knew how to ingratiate himself with his monarch—first Elizabeth and later her successor, James I—which raised his profile and helped make him rich.

The first tetralogy ("first" because it was written first, though chronologically it comes second) consists of *Henry VI, Parts I, II, and III,* and *Richard III.* The last of these ends with the defeat of the villainous King Richard by the Earl of Richmond, soon to be Henry VII, the Tudor king who was Elizabeth's grandfather.

Richard III might have been the end of Shakespeare's British history plays. But the first tetralogy was written soon after the English navy defeated the Spanish Armada, a time when national pride made the dramatization of British history enormously popular, and there was a clamor for more plays in the same genre. But *Richard III* had taken its action very near to the contemporary moment, and continuing forward would mean dealing with people and situations close to home. The risk of a misstep or misreading of the political climate was too great, so Shakespeare went back and wrote a prequel, the second tetralogy: *Richard II, Henry IV, Parts I and II,* and *Henry V.*

Of the four plays in the first tetralogy, only *Richard III* is performed and taught today with any regularity, while all four of the plays in the second tetralogy—especially *Henry IV, Part I* and *Henry V*—are frequently performed and taught. This, I think, is because Shakespeare became a better playwright as he continued writing, an improvement that consisted not only in the way he structured his plots and arranged his characters but also in the way those characters speak to us as real, rounded human beings. Indeed, these two elements go together: more elaborate structures ensure deeper, more interesting and authentic characters.

All the plays in the Henriad have their plots taken from other sources, mostly from Robert Edward Hall's *The Union of the Two Noble and Illustre Families of Lancastre and York* (commonly known as Hall's *Chronicle*) and Rafael Holinshed's *Chronicle of the History of England.* Shakespeare makes no effort to disguise his borrowings. Sometimes, he adds fictional characters, and sometimes he alters the ages and characteristics of historical figures to amplify the drama. Overall, however, he remains faithful to the history as his sources present it. His innovation lies in the words he puts into the mouths of his characters and in what he emphasizes and subordinates. His essential fidelity to the record as he knew it is why nonhistorians so often use these plays as our shorthand source for British monarchical history.

Shakespeare began several of his comedies early in his career, but the plays in the first tetralogy are generally believed to be his first completed works. Of these, the one that I believe marks the ground on which his empathetic imagination would develop is the fourth in the sequence: *Richard III.*

The play's importance lies not in its strength but in its limitation. It offers the outline of what subsequent plays would fill in. This is key to Shakespeare's method: he begins with a sketch or partial treatment of a character in one play and then, because the seed has been planted in his imagination, takes this farther in a later one. Following this method, we can say that *Richard III* offers us, as it did Shakespeare, a kind of negative example of our first encounter with the Other—in this case, a person with a disability. It is an object lesson in how we often respond stereotypically to someone with physical characteristics we consider abnormal.

In the 1950s and 1960s, when I was growing up, people with disabilities were largely kept out of sight in institutions or in their homes. Accommodations for the disabled only began to appear in public spaces in the 1980s, and the Americans with Disabilities Act (ADA) was not passed until 1990. Only in the past fifteen years has the field of Disability Studies gained traction in the university curriculum. It is no wonder, then, that Shakespeare began his writing career with a character like Richard III, whose disability is merely a prop associated with his villainy, not a locus of concern and empathy. What *is* surprising is that after the creation of this character, Shakespeare went on to depict marginality from a far more humane and empathetic perspective. If we consider what Shakespeare *didn't do* with Richard III, we can appreciate what he *did do* with Richard II in the second tetralogy and, even more impressively, with Shylock in *The Merchant of Venice,* written at around the same time.

But let us return to Shakespeare's representation in *Richard III,* where the groundwork was laid. As the play begins, Richard, Duke of Gloucester (whom I will refer to from now on, as Shakespeare does in his character cues, as "Gloucester"), is technically far removed from the throne. His brother Edward IV is king, and both Edward's young sons and Gloucester's older brother Clarence stand ahead in the succession according to the laws of primogeniture that determined who would inherit position and land in England during this period—and indeed, well beyond, into the twentieth century.

Most people for whom something is so out of reach would concentrate their energy and ambition elsewhere. But Gloucester's distance from power seems to be an incentive: the very fact that he is outside the running makes him all the more determined to get what is ostensibly closed to him.

Gloucester is introduced to us at the outset as the victim of a physical disability. Shakespeare derived this fact from one of his sources. Sir Thomas More's *Life of Richard III* is fairly specific in its description: "Richard, the third son [of Richard Duke

of York] . . . [was] little of stature, ill-featured of limbs, crook-
backed, his left shoulder much higher than his right . . ."

Yet Shakespeare does not describe Gloucester from the
outside, the way his source does, but from the inside, as the
character sees himself. This self-description occurs in the opening soliloquy, which begins by first placing us in time. Gloucester explains that the struggle between the houses of Lancaster
and York (known popularly as the War of the Roses) has finally
concluded, putting his brother Edward of York on the throne:

> Now is the winter of our discontent
> Made glorious summer by this son of York. (1.1.1–2)

But where others welcome the advent of peace and the chance
to concentrate on love instead of war, Gloucester announces
that he feels differently. To account for this, he alludes directly
and emphatically—but without precise detail—to the deformed
state of his body:

> But I that am not shaped for sportive tricks
> Nor made to court an amorous looking-glass,
> I that am rudely stamped and want love's majesty
> To strut before a wanton ambling nymph
> I that am curtailed of this fair proportion,
> Cheated of feature by dissembling nature,
> Deformed, unfinished, sent before my time
> Into this breathing world scarce half made up,
> And that so lamely and unfashionable
> That dogs bark at me as I halt by them,
> Why, I, in this weak piping time of peace,
> Have no delight to pass away the time,
> Unless to see my shadow in the sun
> And descant on mine own deformity (1.1.14–27).

He then explains what he *will* do as the logical byproduct of his
deformity:

> And therefore, since I cannot prove a lover
> To entertain these fair well-spoken days,
> I am determined to prove a villain
> And hate the idle pleasures of these days. (1.1.28–31)

This is an extraordinary speech, both in its bitter eloquence (the
four repeated "I's" seem like a cri de coeur of pain in the first
fourteen lines—the length, notably, of a sonnet, though this is
in no strict sense a sonnet) and in the way that it briskly concludes, as if villainy is the only possible course available under
the circumstances.

Gloucester's soliloquy functions as a two-part mechanism:
it opens him to us through its reference to a deformity that should
arouse our pity ("dogs bark at me as I halt by them"); it then
closes him off in its concluding resolution ("And therefore, . . . /
I am determined to prove a villain"). Shakespeare is giving us
the blueprint for a character who could arouse our empathy but
whom the play will not develop in empathetic terms. Instead,
Gloucester becomes an uncomplicated monster. There is never
again a moment when we feel for him.

What drives this character? Ostensibly, a maniacal will to
power. After all, he methodically and cunningly eliminates all
the barriers that block his way to the throne. But the removal of
everyone around him comes to seem gratuitous and, eventually,
counterproductive. It is not a will to power that drives Gloucester but a will to discord and disruption ("to prove [myself] a
villain")—what in Shakespeare's lexicon and that of the Elizabethan worldview more generally is associated with the demonic.

Gloucester's crippled body becomes the outward expression
of a fundamentally evil nature—as though he were plucked from

a medieval morality play where outward form mirrors moral nature. This is an idea adapted, three hundred years later, by Oscar Wilde in *The Picture of Dorian Gray*, though there the assumption is that an evil appearance imprints itself over time on the body if one lives an evil life. Unlike Dorian Gray, Gloucester was born with the deformity that *denotes* his evil.

And yet, for all that he is a kind of emblem of immorality, his opening soliloquy is so powerful that it cannot be entirely erased from our consciousness. Gloucester makes clear in those opening lines that he feels "cheated" as a result of his physical condition. His deformity has denied him his full humanity:

> I that am curtailed of this fair proportion,
> Cheated of feature by dissembling nature,
> Deformed, unfinished, sent before my time
> Into this breathing world scarce half made up. (1.1.18–21)

These lines are so expressive that they hint beyond their literal meaning to the idea that a physical handicap can be an unjust target of discrimination and result in humiliation and ostracism. Perhaps, as my students like to suggest, Gloucester's mother, who hates him justifiably enough in the present, hated him from birth because he did not look like other children. Perhaps the fact that dogs bark at him as he halts by them suggests that men have ridiculed him as well—turning him against them in the way, as we shall see, the Jew in *The Merchant of Venice* is turned against the Christians who abuse him.

But this idea is not developed in the rest of the play. The existential bitterness of the opening soliloquy is never returned to. Even when the ghosts of those whom Gloucester has murdered visit him before his final battle (and who include the young princes whose deaths he ordered without qualm), they have no moral effect. They arouse fear but not guilt.

Gloucester can be seen as the conceptual precursor of Shylock, a destructive character who is nonetheless represented empathetically, as I shall discuss. But it is not until Shakespeare's last play (excepting collaborations) that we see Gloucester's *physical* heir in the character of Caliban in *The Tempest*. Described as a "misshapen knave" and a "monster," Caliban is more literally Other in appearance than Gloucester but not as uninflectedly evil: he has a genuine sense of wonder in the natural world and speaks some of the most beautiful lines in the play—testament to how far Shakespeare has evolved in his empathy for difference.[1]

Many people love *Richard III*. They love the energy with which the protagonist pursues his villainous ends. They love the gruesome piling up of bodies and the ingenuity and chutzpah with which Gloucester carries out his stratagems: courting Lady Anne while she is following the corpse of the husband he himself killed, methodically eliminating both his enemies and his allies out of malice or whim, frantically battling on when his cause is lost. There's something thrilling in the character's mad bravado and unwillingness to cede the day:

> I have set my life upon a cast,
> And I will stand the hazard of the die.
>
> . . .
>
> A horse, a horse, my kingdom for a horse! (5.4.9–10, 13)

The poetry in *Richard III* is also wonderful, though it has, to my mind, a superfluity of rhyme in keeping with the simplistic nature of the characterizations. (There will be less and less rhyme as Shakespeare matures as a playwright.) Gloucester is a role perfectly suited to the scenery-chewing Al Pacino, who has played it in many venues. Pacino even made a documentary about the play, *Looking for Richard*, that does an excellent job sketching in the history and relaying the evil vitality of the character.

I am not saying that *Richard III* isn't a good play; I am saying that it isn't a great one in the way that Shakespeare's plays will become great. It does not feed us emotionally and make us better for having seen or read it. One of my students suggested that the play's popularity may actually derive from this fact. Because it does not make us think or feel too much, it frees us to revel in its protagonist's demonic energy and the mayhem he leaves in his wake.

Gloucester's disability both isolates him and becomes the emblem of his isolation. Because he never exists in a relationship, he never appears to be fully human. This distinguishes him from subsequent Shakespeare characters.

The nineteenth-century poet and critic Samuel Taylor Coleridge referred to Iago in *Othello* as a "motiveless malignity." But Iago is not motiveless, as I shall discuss below. His anger at Othello ("I hate the Moor") gives his villainy its focus, but it also engenders a degree of identification and even empathy in us if we read closely and without preconception. Other villains are similarly deepened by having antagonists and consorts against or with whom they can be developed: Cassius has Brutus; Macbeth has Lady Macbeth; Edmund has Edward and, in some sense, Goneril and Regan; Hamlet has Ophelia, his mother, and most of all his divided self. This abrasion of the self with something outside or within it is missing in Gloucester. In this, he resembles Dostoyevsky's Underground Man, cut off from everything but his own embittered consciousness. Dostoyevsky's character is a commentary on social alienation, but Gloucester is about nothing but devious and bloodless plotting. He is a popcorn villain, a vehicle for the representation of evil as sheer entertainment. I am reminded of James Bond villains—fun to watch but with no psychological complexity worth considering. In *Richard III*, Shakespeare has not yet created a character who, though radically Other, can elicit our empathy. He will do this in his next history play, *Richard II*.

3

Richard II, Henry IV,
and *Henry V*

Beginning

ichard II, the first play in the second tetralogy, marks
a beginning for Shakespeare in the empathetic portrayal of character. It takes us back in historical time,
but it is the work of a more seasoned playwright.
Shakespeare had by now written some ten plays as opposed to
the mere three that precede *Richard III*.

Both Richard II and Richard III are destructive personalities. But where Richard III is never given a proper antagonist
to deepen him as a character, Richard II is matched by his
cousin, Henry Bullingbrook. Bullingbrook appears in the first
scene of the play leveling an accusation of treason against another character, Thomas Mowbray. This accusation is soon
revealed to be a pretense—a veiled threat to Richard himself,
in whose service Mowbray has acted. The upstart cousin is, in
actuality, challenging his king.

Even before this antagonism becomes explicit, however, it is foreshadowed in the contrasting language of the two characters. Richard's speech is flowery and vague; Bullingbrook's is direct and certain. Every student I have ever taught has initially disliked Richard and been impressed by Bullingbrook. But the play moves steadily toward a complication of this response as these characters become affected by changing circumstances.

Qualities that had constituted Richard's unlikableness at the beginning make him more likable—or at least more humanly poignant—once things begin to look dire for him. And the emphatic moral justification that had made Bullingbrook seem heroic—his promise that he has returned from exile to recover his family's land ("I come but for my own")—once breached, begins to make us question both his original statement of intention and his humanity.

It seems worth noting that about a year before the writing of this play Shakespeare had become one of eight "sharers"—those splitting profits and debts—in the theatrical troupe known as the Lord Chamberlain's Men. This involved a change in his status from an itinerant actor and freelance playwright to a committed and financially invested member of a group consisting of men of differing ages, backgrounds, personalities, and physical types—the diversity needed for playing a wide range of characters. In assuming his new role, Shakespeare would also have had to address questions and controversies arising from his plays. *Richard II,* for example, was written before the Essex Rebellion, an unsuccessful effort to overthrow Queen Elizabeth. It could have been viewed as treasonous. Shakespeare's diplomatic skills would have been tested in diffusing such suspicion. (Indeed, after the rebellion, he excised the usurpation scene from the play, at least during Elizabeth's lifetime.)

In other words, Shakespeare's position in his troupe would have entailed more engagement with diverse issues and personalities and made him more attuned to difference.[1] The change would have contributed to an evolution in his creative process, from projecting what he felt and thought onto others to imagining what others felt and thought. The result would make it impossible to create another static villain like Gloucester in *Richard III.*

Shakespeare's more complex rendering of Richard II was also helped by his having hit on a conflict that could encapsulate more than a particular clash between a king and his disgruntled and ambitious cousin. He could enfold into the drama a historical shift—from the medieval past to the modern present, from a universe whose meanings are out of reach of human beings (the Divine Right associated with Richard II's rule) to one in which the stratagems of will and ingenuity (Bullingbrook's qualities) can effect change.

In act 4, the Duke of Carlisle explains the dangers that will result if Richard is usurped by Bullingbrook. This is the oracular voice of the play:

> And if you crown him let me prophesy:
> The blood of English shall manure the ground
> And future ages groan for this foul act.
> Peace shall go sleep with Turks and infidels,
> And in this seat of peace tumultuous wars
> Shall kin with kin and kind with kind confound.
> . . .
> Oh, if you raise this house against this house
> It will the woefullest division prove
> That ever fell upon this cursèd earth.
> Prevent it, resist it, let it not be so,
> Lest child, child's children, cry against you woe. (4.1.136–
> 141, 145–149)

The many monosyllabic words, the rudimentary sense of history (from "child" to "child's children"), the warning against a fundamental violation of nature ("Shall kin with kin and kind with kind confound"), and the rhyming final couplet all support a simple but powerful argument.

Once the usurpation happens, we see its effects on the particular individual, Richard himself, for whom the loss of the throne is experienced not in the sweeping societal terms that Carlisle describes, but in humiliating personal ones:

> Alack, why am I sent for to a king
> Before I have shook off the regal thoughts
> Wherewith I reigned? I hardly yet have learned
> To insinuate, flatter, bow and bend my knee.
> Give sorrow leave awhile to tutor me
> To this submission. (4.1.162–167)

In his later, more famous speech at the end of act 5, Richard's sense of loss remains personal but now encompasses a new sense of shared humanity:

> Thus play I in one person many people,
> And none contented. Sometimes am I king,
> Then treasons make me wish myself a beggar,
> And so I am. Then crushing penury
> Persuades me I was better when a king,
> Then am I kinged again, and by and by
> Think that I am unkinged by Bullingbrook,
> And straight am nothing. But whate'er I be
> Nor I nor any man that but man is
> With nothing shall be pleased till he be eased
> With being nothing. (5.5.31–41)

This is a universal insight grown out of personal suffering—and it is suffering that we can not only pity but also, if we are philosophical about our own fate, personally understand. We may rationalize the ups and downs of our lives, but we still know that we ultimately face the singular, inescapable reality of death, a tragic destiny that we share with all humanity.

Such a perspective is alien to Bullingbrook. He is a man of action, not a philosopher, and unlikely to ever become one, even on his deathbed, which we shall see him occupy in *Henry IV, Part II.* His success is built out of a meritocratic concept of power. If he is not a good person, he is, at least, a competent one, a strategist who understands how the world works and judiciously positions himself to take advantage of this. If we look back to *Richard III,* that stylized but diverting play, we see that the idea of strategy had figured heavily there, too: Gloucester was relentlessly strategic, moving against enemies and perceived enemies with an ingenious determination to get what he wanted. But his actions were without context. We could not empathize with him because we could not situate him with respect to any other person, no less ourselves. Bullingbrook, by contrast, stands for something, even if he is also clearly out for himself. He rallies the other noblemen behind him because they see their interests in his. We can also see our interests in his. Most of us prefer to act and be judged based on what we do rather than on what we were born into. This draws us to Bullingbrook as co-conspirators even as it makes us question, through the increasingly pitiful situation of Richard II, what must be sacrificed in the process.

By using this larger historical scheme to situate his conflict, Shakespeare found a way to create more nuanced characters. Richard II and Bullingbrook each represent both positive and negative values. Richard II's divine claim to the throne has advantages: it is predictable and reassuring to know that the overall structure of things will remain in place, even with a capricious monarch who might sacrifice an individual or two to his whims. But Bullingbrook's merit-based claim also has appeal; it reflects greater fairness and a potential for dynamic progress. These positive and negative elements are enfolded into the characterizations, with the result that each evokes mixed feelings.

When I teach *Richard II,* I find my class is similarly divided in its loyalties. Students determined to follow family expectations tend to oppose Bullingbrook, whereas those who have diverged from what is expected by, say, choosing a career trajectory or unconventional major (English literature over pre-med, for example) tend to support him. In some cases, belonging to a close extended family can make students more attached to a traditional hierarchy and thus more sympathetic to Richard; in others, it can make them more determined to strike out on their own and support Bullingbrook. I am always surprised by how Shakespeare can help explain and clarify my students' beliefs, and how often they can find support for opposing positions in his work.

Richard II is also, of course, a deeply political play and leads inevitably to discussion of the benefits and costs of social disruption—of conservative versus progressive thinking—a question that the remaining plays in the second tetralogy continue to explore.

The characters of Richard II and Bullingbrook are so adeptly positioned to complicate each other that we might wonder where Shakespeare could go from here. How could he develop characters who would build on this rich and interesting structure? Yet the three remaining plays in the second tetralogy are, in their ways, more complex character studies than this one.

It is an astonishing feat of imagination that allows Shakespeare to shift from two more or less equally positioned antagonists in *Richard II* to three figures in tension whose positioning is unequal or, one could say, staggered with respect to one another in *Henry IV, Part I*. I am referring to the relationship set up between Bullingbrook (now Henry IV) and his son Prince Hal, and between Prince Hal and his elderly dissipated friend Sir John Falstaff.

The triangle here has Hal situated between two father figures, each pulling him in a different direction. Henry IV's world is formal and public; Falstaff's is playful and domestic. These worlds are not only opposed to each other; they are centers of conflict in their own right. Hal must battle the king as he must battle Falstaff, not to literally defeat either but to alleviate their power over him and to incorporate some of their values into himself. Instead of the historical structure of past versus present that was central to *Richard II,* Shakespeare now presents us with contrasting worldviews in the present: work versus play, power versus pleasure, action versus rhetoric. These structures of conflict are replete with contradiction and paradox. The result is a character in Hal who is also more complicated than either his father, the former upstart Bullingbrook, now King Henry IV, or his father's predecessor, the usurped Richard II.

By the same token, *Henry IV, Part I* reinserts a structure familiar from *Richard II*. It introduces a direct foil to Hal in Northumberland's son Harry Percy, known as Hotspur. The relationship between Hal and Hotspur recapitulates the conflict connected to the historical loyalties of that earlier play. In Holinshed's *Chronicles,* from which the plot is borrowed, Hotspur is a generation older than Prince Hal. But Shakespeare revises Hotspur's age to make them contemporaries. This produces the symmetry needed for Hal's character development.

Northumberland and Worcester, Hotspur's father and uncle, helped Bullingbrook depose Richard II. They now seek to oust Henry for not rewarding them adequately. But Hotspur, a generation younger, had no part in that earlier usurpation. He can therefore credibly decry the killing of Richard as a crime against God, while his father and uncle (who had ignored the Duke of Carlisle's warning in the earlier play) cannot.

As a supporter of older values, Hotspur places himself in opposition to Henry IV, but also, more dramatically, to Prince Hal, who, as a strategist more subtle than his father, wants to appear as the legitimate heir without discrediting the illegitimate means by which his father gained the throne. Hotspur is transparent and upright where Hal is covert and devious; Hal's most revealing speeches are in soliloquy; Hotspur's are in bursts of temper in public forums. That Henry IV wishes that Hotspur, the old world chivalric character, were his son demonstrates that he has come to value the orderly past that he helped destroy but which he now has a stake in maintaining in its reconstituted form:

> O that it could be proved
> That some night-tripping fairy had exchanged
> In cradle-clothes our children where they lay,
> And called mine Percy, his Plantagenet! (1.1.85–88)

But Hal is unlike his father in being a genuinely new kind of character—one who points us toward the divided self dramatically on display in *Hamlet.* We glimpse this new aspect of character at the end of act 1, scene 2, when Hal, in soliloquy, claims that he is biding his time, playing at debauchery with his low-life friends in order to more dramatically reveal his reformation at a later date:

> I know you all, and will a while uphold
> The unyoked humour of your idleness.
> Yet herein will I imitate the sun,

Who doth permit the base contagious clouds
To smother up his beauty from the world,
That when he please again to be himself,
Being wanted, he may be more wondered at
By breaking through the foul and ugly mists
Of vapours that did seem to strangle him.
If all the year were playing holidays,
To sport would be as tedious as to work;
But when they seldom come, they wished-for come,
And nothing pleaseth but rare accidents.
So, when this loose behaviour I throw off,
And pay the debt I never promisèd,
By how much better than my word I am,
By so much shall I falsify men's hopes.
And like bright metal on a sullen ground,
My reformation, glitt'ring o'er my fault,
Shall show more goodly, and attract more eyes
Than that which hath no foil to set it off.
I'll so offend, to make offence a skill,
Redeeming time when men think least I will.
(1.2.174–196)

The soliloquy bears an affinity to Gloucester's at the beginning of *Richard III*. Again, it is Shakespeare's habit to reuse patterns of rhetoric and ideas in new contexts: the speech shows calculation and an arrogant disdain for others. But unlike Gloucester, who stated his villainous motives directly, Hal's motives are not exactly villainous; indeed, they are not entirely clear. Does he seek power or respectability, the love of the people or of his father? Is he sincere in what he is saying or is he rationalizing his behavior to himself? My students are always fascinated by this speech—it is so deliciously adolescent. It annoys some, who find it smug and cold, while it impresses others, who find it cool

and smart. The very fact that it can evoke such different responses is part of its complexity and originality. Clearly, Shakespeare is trying to do something new with this character.
Moreover, Hal is speaking in a new context—as the son of a
king who also happens to be a usurper. As such, he is burdened
with a public responsibility and a political challenge. None of
this operates for Gloucester, who exists only in the bitterness
generated by his deformity.

Eventually, Hal kills Hotspur, and when he does we see
more clearly the split in his character. After the duel, he pays
tribute to the man he has killed, then immediately retracts that
tribute:

> This earth that bears thee dead
> Bears not alive so stout a gentleman.
> If thou wert sensible of courtesy
> I should not make so dear a show of zeal. (5.4.91–94)

The awareness of a double position—as a private man mourn-
ing a worthy antagonist and as a public man who needs that
antagonist dead—is succinctly presented.

The divided self that appears in nascent form in Prince Hal
is extended further in *Henry V* when the prince becomes king.
Now the tension is amplified between a public man whose image is paramount and a private man who seeks release from the
demands of a public role. This split self is dramatized at the
beginning of act 4, as Hal, now King Henry V, muses to himself
while wandering in disguise through his soldiers' camp before
the Battle of Agincourt, the determining battle in the war against
France that he has initiated to solidify his reign:

> What infinite heart's ease must kings neglect
> That private men enjoy?

And what have kings that privates have not too,
Save ceremony, save general ceremony?

He goes on to explain that "ceremony" is an inadequate reward
for the burdens of kingship:

'Tis not the balm, the sceptre and the ball,
The sword, the mace, the crown imperial,
The intertissued robe of gold and pearl,
The farcèd title running 'fore the king,
The throne he sits on, nor the tide of pomp
That beats upon the high shore of this world;
No, not all these, thrice-gorgeous ceremony,
Not all these, laid in bed majestical,
Can sleep so soundly as the wretched slave
Who, with a body filled and vacant mind,
Gets him to rest, crammed with distressful bread;

In the end, he concludes, the slave is to be envied over the king:

And but for ceremony such a wretch,
Winding up days with toil and nights with sleep,
Had the forehand and vantage of a king.
The slave, a member of the country's peace,
Enjoys it, but in gross brain little wots
What watch the king keeps to maintain the peace,
Whose hours the peasant best advantages. (4.1.214–217,
238–248, 256–262)

We are induced to feel something for Henry here, burdened as
he is by the trappings of "ceremony," unable to enjoy the peace-
ful sleep he attributes to the slave and the peasant. But our
empathy is limited to how much we are moved by whining

privilege and stage fright. Henry V is not experiencing genuine existential anguish; he is not questioning his core sense of self or seriously contemplating an alternative course of action.

This will change in the great tragedies *Othello, Lear,* and *Macbeth;* will reach its apotheosis in *Hamlet;* and become the impetus for a new kind of heroism in *Antony and Cleopatra.* Yet the beginning of the divided self is certainly on display in *Henry V,* the play that seems to have set its creator's imagination working in a direction he would be compelled to pursue further.

In the process of writing the eight plays that make up the Henriad, Shakespeare addressed the idea of change in two overlapping forms: historical change, involving shifting regimes; and existential change, involving individual destinies. The plays are both political and personal. They are also familial: everyone in this vast historical drama is related to everyone else. If the noblemen and women are engaged in political rivalry, they are also engaged in the age-old rivalry of blood relations, something that makes them profoundly familiar. My students invariably see themselves in Hal as he struggles with his father, his friend Falstaff, and his rival Hotspur. They understand the stress that comes with his finally assuming the responsibilities of kingship, which translates for them into the responsibilities of adulthood that lie ahead as they approach graduation. To teach *Henry IV, Parts I and II* and *Henry V* to college students is to teach these plays to an ideal audience—young people about to be thrust into a challenging world in which much will be expected of them. It is a world they both wish to enter and are petrified of entering.

When Shakespeare completed *Henry V,* he had already written the first tetralogy that chronologically followed it. This must have brought home to him, as it does to us, how easily the individual disappears into the historical record and how that record depends on those who have the power to represent it for posterity.

This insight returns, in morally distilled form, in the last plays of Shakespeare's career, referred to by scholars as the Romances. In these plays, history in its particulars is bypassed for the schematics of change. Many of the themes and character tropes of earlier work are placed into a generalized long view. Tragedy is subsumed within a larger philosophical vision of renewal and regeneration, and history is reduced to the bare bones of generational succession.

This triumph of perspective can be seen as the final stop for a playwright who began imagining the Other in the early histories and continued from there to develop an ever-widening, more empathetic perspective on the human condition. In the following chapters I shall trace the path that led to this point.

4

The Merchant of Venice

Blueprint

As with many Shakespeare's plays, the central plot of *The Merchant of Venice* existed in an earlier source, Giovanni Fiorentino's *Il Pecorone* (The Simpleton), an Italian story written in 1378 and published in 1558. Since it had not been translated, Shakespeare no doubt read it in Italian, which, along with French, he probably knew moderately well. He borrowed many elements from *Il Pecorone*, including a Jewish moneylender who demands a pound of flesh when a loan is not paid on time and a woman who disguises herself as a lawyer to save the man who received the loan.

The fact that Shakespeare borrowed from other sources has often befuddled my students. They exist in a culture committed to "originality" and are continually faced with menacing warnings on their course syllabuses about what plagiarism will do to their grade. I suspect that they initially think less of Shakespeare for having stolen his plots and characters.

The conventional stance on Shakespeare's borrowing is that there were no copyright laws at that time. Everyone took from everyone else, and no one was accountable in the way we are today. But this suggests that Shakespeare and his contemporaries were naive or primitive in their creativity, and that current practices are more enlightened and supportive of greatness. This conclusion strikes me as wrong-headed. Shakespeare's borrowing was not a benighted maneuver that diminished his originality, but an advantage that was instrumental in feeding his genius and making him the writer he became.[1]

In this respect, it seems apt that he began his career with the Henriad. The historical characters and events in the various chronicles he consulted were the materials he needed to animate his imagination. And having begun with historical sources based on real people and events, he could proceed to do the same using fictional sources. Shakespeare did not just add poetical language to what he appropriated; he brought complexity of thought and feeling to those borrowed plots and characters. Indeed, I see this as a necessary process in his creative and moral development: he *needed* someone to have traversed the ground before him so that he could then revisit it and infuse it with new and, ultimately, empathetic meaning.

This method of reclamation seems to me especially applicable to *The Merchant of Venice*. The plot that Shakespeare happened upon in *Il Pecorone* led to a pivotal moment of creativity in his career. It afforded him the opportunity to develop his source into something far more rich and strange, and then carry the elements addressed in this play forward into later plays. The plot of the bloodthirsty moneylending Jew was a trope that inspired—I would even say "inflamed"—Shakespeare's imagination and, having been dealt with in *Merchant,* it remained an incitement that led to the creation of Othello and Lear. Just as he borrowed from other sources and injected thought and feeling into that material, he similarly returned to themes and characters in his own work and infused them with greater thought and feeling as he matured as a playwright.

The Merchant of Venice is, in my opinion, Shakespeare's most important play from a structural point of view. The sheer range of opportunities for complexity that it generates is unparalleled in his canon. It introduces three outsider characters—a Jew, a gay man, and a woman—and creates empathy for them to various degrees. It is a revolutionary play in this respect, though it is also one whose radical aspects can be glossed over or misinterpreted.

The play has had its advocates over the years, and sympathetic representations of Shylock date back to the nineteenth century. It is not possible to say if such representations existed in the performances of Shakespeare's day—one has to wonder about how the actor in his troupe interpreted the role under his direction. But it has not received the recognition it deserves for its groundbreaking aspects until recently, possibly as a result of Al Pacino's 2004 movie version, the product of a cultural climate more sympathetic to the representation of the Other than ever before.

I confess that early in my career, I avoided teaching the play. As a Jewish professor with a large contingent of Catholic students, I felt that the character of Shylock would raise questions that I was not prepared to answer. Yet when I eventually tackled it, the experience surprised me. I found that it contained the very ingredients needed to defend against anti-Semitic thinking, though in a nuanced rather than a simplistic, finger-wagging way.

Recently, however, a new problem has emerged in teaching this play. I have had to deal with students who refuse to see Shylock as a villain—who *over*-empathize with him. As much as I understand this impulse, I find it almost as disturbing as an anti-Semitic reading. To see Shylock as heroic is as wrong-headed as to see him as an uninflected villain. For in no sense is the elevation of victimhood consistent with Shakespeare's empathetic imagination. Despite the abuse Shylock suffers as a Jew in a Christian society—and in large part, *because* of what that abuse has done to him—he remains the villain of the piece. That he *is* the villain is what makes our empathy for him so complicated and important.

The Merchant of Venice begins, significantly, not with Shylock but with the merchant of the title, Antonio, who is shown speaking to his friends about his feelings of unfocused depression:

> In sooth I know not why I am so sad.
> It wearies me, you say it wearies you;
> But how I caught it, found it, or came by it,
> What stuff 'tis made of, whereof it is born,
> I am to learn.
> And such a want-wit sadness makes of me,
> That I have much ado to know myself. (1.1.1–7)

This is a strange, off-kilter beginning. One could say that it is meant to foreshadow Antonio's later scrape with death. But it is also suggestive of a covert love story. Antonio's friend Solanio, who is addressed in these opening lines, responds with the suggestion that he must be in love. Antonio curtly denies this just as his best friend, Bassanio, enters the scene. The passage, in other words, is a brilliant feat of insinuation. It suggests from the opening exchange that Antonio *is* in love, and then, with the appearance of Bassanio, shows us his love object. As the play proceeds and Antonio seems to be almost eager to martyr himself on behalf of his friend, this supposition is reinforced.

I see precedents for Antonio's covert homosexual longing in several of Shakespeare's works which, I surmise, preceded or were written in close proximity to the completion of *The Merchant of Venice*. First, the sonnets, or at least the first 126 (of 154), which Shakespeare addressed to a beautiful and noble young man, generally thought to be the Earl of Southampton. These poems, probably composed in the early 1590s, express a quality of lovelorn wistfulness very much like Antonio's state of mind at the beginning of *The Merchant of Venice*.

The second hint is from *Richard II,* when Bullingbrook suggests the homosexual involvement of Richard with his "favorites," Bushy and Green, part of a group of sycophants with whom he has surrounded himself:

> You have in manner with your sinful hours
> . . .
> Broke the possession of a royal bed,
> And stained the beauty of a fair queen's cheeks
> With tears drawn from her eyes by your foul wrongs.
> (3.1.11, 13–15)

The hint is never taken up in the play, and it is easy to imagine the strategically savvy Bullingbrook concocting a rumor of this sort to support his interests. Even so, the statement is suggestive of a private Richard that conflicts with the public role he has had to assume since childhood (he has been king since the age of ten). We do, ultimately, see a private Richard with a capacity to suffer and think deeply when he is stripped of power and authority, but the homosexual insinuation raised earlier is not revisited in this context.

The third and most structurally significant hint for the character of Antonio comes from *Romeo and Juliet,* probably written not long before *The Merchant of Venice*. It is present in

Romeo's witty and imaginative friend Mercutio, who dies when he takes the place of Romeo in a duel with Juliet's cousin Tybalt. It seems to me logical to see Mercutio as the precursor to Antonio. Romeo's responsibility for his friend's death disturbs him, but his concern dissipates as his resulting problems with Juliet take precedence. In other words, the feeling of guilt for the death of a beloved friend is both suggested and shunted aside, and this, I believe, explains the return to a more direct and thorough treatment of a similar situation involving an intimate male relationship in *The Merchant of Venice*.

While Mercutio is inserted into the play as a secondary, quasi-clownish character and is eliminated halfway through, Antonio begins the play on a sober note and becomes the hinge upon which a potentially tragic outcome turns. It is Antonio's act of generosity toward Bassanio, taking out the loan from Shylock and pledging a pound of his own flesh as bond, that sets the plot in motion. In the source, *Il Pecorone*, the Antonio character is the godfather of the Bassanio character and has a lesser role. But we must assume that Shakespeare wants to make Antonio central to his story for two reasons: because he is intent on creating a covert love story between Antonio and Bassanio and because he wants to situate Antonio as a structural counterpart to Shylock. Both are outsider characters, left alone at the end of the play—loose ends, so to speak, that Shakespeare will feel obliged to take up again in later plays.

Antonio's issues as an outsider are more vague and covert than Shylock's, allowing him to be taken at face value by those who choose to see him as simply a loyal friend and benefactor. But there is little doubt that more is going on, because the suggestion that Antonio is in love opens the play and also because he pushes Bassanio into the difficult situation with the rings (to be discussed later). It therefore seems irrefutable to me and, I should note, even more to my students that Antonio is in love with Bassanio; this is why he is willing to place himself on the line for his friend and why, eventually, he will seem so resigned to die on his behalf.

While Antonio and Bassanio represent a covert love story, the play also features an explicit, if arguably more superficial, one. Bassanio claims to be in love with Portia, an heiress living at her estate, Belmont. He needs Antonio's money to travel there to win her. Antonio's ships, containing all his wealth, are away at sea, so he borrows from Shylock to help Bassanio in his courtship.

At Belmont, Portia has been instructed by her late father's will to demand that those who want to marry her be presented with three riddles affixed to three caskets, made of gold, silver, and lead, respectively. The suitor who properly interprets the riddles and chooses the correct casket will win her hand. After two suitors pick the wrong caskets, Portia, who from the outset has inexplicably favored Bassanio, provides him with hints so that he answers correctly. (Her relief when her first suitor, the dark-skinned Prince of Morocco, fails to guess correctly will become relevant later when I discuss *Othello*.)

No sooner is the marriage between Portia and Bassanio accomplished than news arrives that Antonio's ships have been delayed at sea, making it impossible for him to repay his debt on time. Bassanio also learns that Shylock is steadfast in demanding the agreed-upon penalty: a pound of Antonio's flesh. Bassanio and his friend Gratiano must therefore hurry back to Venice to try to save him.

In a move of unusual whimsy and oddity that Shakespeare borrowed from his Italian source, Portia proceeds to disguise herself as Balthazar, a precocious male lawyer, and with her maid Nerissa disguised as her assistant follows Bassanio to Venice to plead Antonio's case.

The disguised Portia ends up saving Antonio, which, one could say, makes her responsible for thwarting the machinations of not only Shylock but Antonio himself, for whom death would have assured his enshrinement in the regard of the man he loves. As it is, after the trial is concluded, Antonio supports Bassanio's giving up the ring that Portia, disguised as Balthazar, demands as payment—the ring previously given to Bassanio by Portia to seal their marriage. This act symbolically places the male friendship above the marriage.

But if Antonio lurks around the edges of the play in unconscious league with Shylock to effect the masochistic destiny he may secretly desire, Shylock stands increasingly at the center. He is a villain whose lines not only explain his villainy but elicit our empathy—at least insofar as we attend to those lines closely.

As with Richard II, our feeling for Shylock gains in strength and complexity over the course of the play. His terms for the contract with Antonio over the loan seem initially like a jest— though with an ominous undertone. It is clear from the beginning that he deeply resents the merchant on two counts:

> I hate him for he is a Christian;
> But more, for that in low simplicity
> He lends out money gratis, and brings down
> The rate of usance here with us in Venice. (1.3.35–38)

But there is pathos to Shylock, even here, as he goes to great pains to rationalize his usury by way of an Old Testament example involving the trading of ewes between Jacob and Laban. The example is hard to follow, and yet its logic is infallible, in keeping with the character's fastidious style of speech and thought. His painstaking justification for moneylending may also have significance when we consider that Shakespeare's father lent out money at interest and was probably brought up on charges for the practice. (Shakespeare himself is said to have engaged in moneylending as part of his entrepreneurial activities, both in London and in his native Stratford-on-Avon.)

Shylock's hatred of Antonio as a Christian may initially seem a function of religious difference, but it soon becomes clear that this hatred is fueled by the way this man, *as* a Christian, treats him *as* a Jew. This is elucidated when he describes how Antonio has behaved toward him in their previous encounters:

> Signor Antonio, many a time and oft
> In the Rialto you have rated me
> About my moneys and my usances.
> Still have I borne it with a patient shrug
> For suff'rance is the badge of all our tribe.
> You call me misbeliever, cut-throat dog,
> And spit upon my Jewish gaberdine,
> And all for use of that which is mine own.
> Well then, it now appears you need my help:
> Go to, then, you come to me, and you say,
> "Shylock, we would have monies"—you say so,
> You that did void your rheum upon my beard,
> And foot me as you spurn a stranger cur
> Over your threshold: monies is your suit.
> What should I say to you? Should I not say
> "Hath a dog money? Is it possible
> A cur can lend three thousand ducats?" Or
> Shall I bend low, and in a bondman's key,
> With bated breath and whisp'ring humbleness,
> Say this:
> "Fair sir, you spat on me on Wednesday last,
> You spurn'd me such a day, another time
> You called me dog; and for these courtesies
> I'll lend you thus much monies." (1.3.99–122)

The speech is direct and powerful, full of minute examples that give us a visceral understanding of Shylock's humiliation and the hypocrisy involved in Antonio's request to borrow from him now. Its presence seems designed to make us understand the animus of the character. Shakespeare takes pains to give Shylock a mannered, archaic turn of speech, one that underlines both his scrupulous logic and his Otherness. (The alien *style* of the speech can also explain why its pathos could be obscured by an actor intent on showcasing the character's alien nature and, hence, his villainy.)

If Gloucester's abusers were dogs ("dogs bark at me as I halt by them"), Shylock is treated *like* a dog by Antonio. This generous friend to Bassanio has no compassion for an individual who operates outside his particular social, commercial, and religious circle—no awareness of the illogic as well as the inhumanity of his treatment of another human being. Indeed, Antonio proudly owns his behavior and boasts that he has no intention of changing it:

> I am as like to call thee so again,
> To spit on thee again, to spurn thee too.
> If thou wilt lend this money, lend it not
> As to thy friends, for when did friendship take
> A breed for barren metal of his friend?
> But lend it rather to thine enemy,
> Who if he break, thou mayst with better face
> Exact the penalty. (1.3.123–130)

The callousness and meanness of this speech are astonishing, and my students reading it today seem incited to want to take Antonio's pound of flesh on the spot.

Shylock initially seems to slough off Antonio's cruel response, agreeing to a loan, as he puts it, "in a merry sport" that involves the following terms:

> If you repay me not on such a day,
> In such a place, such sum or sums as are
> Expressed in the condition, let the forfeit
> Be nominated for an equal pound
> Of your fair flesh, to be cut off and taken
> In what part of your body pleaseth me. (1.3.140–145)

Shakespeare has now set the stage for what will transpire, making us feel the force of the injustice perpetrated against Shylock, the depth of his resentment, and Antonio's inability to understand the injustice or the resentment.

And yet Shylock's resolution to exact the penalty can be said to be solidified only later, with the elopement of his daughter Jessica with a Christian. When Shylock cries out, "My daughter! O, my ducats! O, my daughter!" he is lamenting the loss of the two things that constitute his identity: his one blood relationship and his wealth, which his daughter steals from him when she elopes. The material loss includes the revelation that among the stolen goods is the ring he received from his dead wife and that Jessica has traded for a monkey:

> it was my
> turquoise, I had it of Leah when I was a bachelor. I
> would not have given it for a wilderness of monkeys.
> (3.1.101–103)

The ring, like the ring that Portia gives Bassanio in act 3, is the seal of love and the symbol of marriage. Shylock got the ring from his now deceased wife. The fact that Leah's ring (the use of the proper name is poignant) was not only stolen but traded for a monkey places its worth below that of a human creature. Antonio treated Shylock like a dog; now his wife's ring is traded for a monkey. One cannot help but feel the degradation involved here—to empathize with Shylock's pain and humiliation. It is worth noting that the sequence involving a daughter's elopement and thievery from her father was borrowed from Anthony Monday's *Zelauto: The Fountain of Fame* (1580), but in the source the characters are not Jewish. By adapting this element to his plot, Shakespeare was adding a detail that further humanized his Jewish villain.

For it is after Jessica's betrayal that Shylock expounds upon his hatred of Antonio in dramatic detail—a speech that prepares us for his determination to exact revenge at all costs:

> He hath disgraced me, and hindered me half a million, laughed at my losses, mocked at my gains, scorned my nation, thwarted my bargains, cooled my friends, heated mine enemies—and what's his reason? I am a Jew. Hath not a Jew eyes? Hath not a Jew hands, organs, dimensions, senses, affections, passions? Fed with the same food, hurt with the same weapons, subject to the same diseases, healed by the same means, warmed and cooled by the same winter and summer as a Christian is? If you prick us, do we not bleed? If you tickle us, do we not laugh? If you poison us, do we not die? And if you wrong us, shall we not revenge? If we are like you in the rest, we will resemble you in that. If a Jew wrong a Christian, what is his humility? Revenge. If a Christian wrong a Jew, what should his sufferance be by Christian example? Why, revenge! The villainy you teach me, I will execute, and it shall go hard but I will better the instruction. (3.1.46–62)

The speech deserves comparison to some elements in *Richard III*. In act 3 of that play, Gloucester blames others for his deformity—accusing his brother's wife and mistress of

> damnèd witchcraft . . .
> Upon my body . . .
>   . . .
> Look how I am bewitched. Behold, mine arm
> Is like a blasted sapling, withered up. (3.4.60–61, 67–68)

The speech in this early play is meant to be ridiculous—an example of Gloucester's daffily strategic mind that uses everything, including his deformity, as a way of clearing away anyone he thinks might impede his progress. But I suspect that Shakespeare, happening upon this maneuver in Hall's *Chronicle* (where it appears almost verbatim), was spurred to think more deeply about blame in other circumstances of marginality where it might be justified.

Unlike Gloucester's absurd argument against his enemies, Shylock's argument seems logical and convincing to most people who read it closely today—though this was not always the case, as I shall discuss.

Shylock claims to have been made a villain not by witchcraft but by the abrasions of living in Venetian society—by the very Christians with whom he does business on a regular basis and whose religion preaches mercy and compassion. Antonio, elsewhere represented as a true gentleman and a loyal friend to Bassanio, has, as we have seen, made a point of demeaning Shylock in his commercial dealings and hence is most responsible for fueling his murderous resentment.

The pathos of Shylock's speech grows as one concentrates on it; we understand the pain of being thwarted in every sense of the word—monetarily but also in self-respect and personal dignity. Shylock admits that he has no concrete use for Antonio's pound of flesh ("What's that good for?" asks Salarino; "To bait fish withal," responds Shylock). This anticipates the later statement by Lear in an entirely different context: "Reason not the need." In

Shylock's case, the need is to salve a wound to his humanity—the definition, one could argue, of the often impractical "need" that fuels vengeance.

But to see this requires not only attention to the lines spoken by the character but receptiveness to empathetic feeling. A good actor who wants to highlight Shylock's villainy can obscure the full force of the words and can perform the play in the manner of a Christian morality tale in which Shylock's killing of Antonio repeats the original alleged "killing" of Christ by the Jews.

Shylock, moreover, is a usurer, and usury is represented in the New Testament (and by Antonio inside the play) as a degenerate occupation. Early in my career I found that few of my students could follow Shylock's biblical justification for his trade (or cared to equate his work with their future careers in finance). As my university became more diverse, however, Shylock's position as a marginal figure began to be noted and appreciated. This serves as a testimonial on behalf of diversity as a motor for empathy. Surround yourself with like-minded people and you are likely to feel only for those like you; diversify your surroundings and your range of feeling expands.

Recently, as I noted earlier, my students' tendency has been to over-empathize with Shylock, with some seeing him less as the twisted product of anti-Semitism than as a righteous scourge on behalf of his people. To kill Antonio, these students have argued, is to rid Venice of an abuser who deserves to die. In the face of this argument, I feel I am reenacting Portia's role in another register: calling for my class to be merciful toward Antonio.

The courtroom scene in act 4 is the culminating dramatic action of the play. It brings together Shylock, Antonio, and Portia (disguised as Balthazar)—all three marginal figures with respect to the society in which they find themselves. Each is in some way supportive of that society: Antonio through material transaction; Shylock through monetary transaction; Portia through legal transaction. The presentation of these characters in a setting presided over by the governor of the region could be read as a dramatic demonstration of how marginal characters serve as the hidden foundation for social functioning. Again, it seems to me that Shakespeare, by arranging things in such a way, is bringing this fact home to his audience and also to himself—a cue, as it were, to ideas that he will feel compelled to develop in subsequent plays.

Portia saves Antonio and destroys Shylock, a trade-off that may suggest that marginal figures are often saved at the expense of one another—that there is only so much room for mercy in a society based on a zero-sum game. Portia has, in fact, pleaded with Shylock to let "mercy season justice" and been rejected. But she herself will not do so when she has the opportunity to exercise mercy. Thus, we watch these marginal figures dig in their heels, driven by bitterness and righteous indignation, determined to impose justice as they understand it. Their actions help us see that justice is a construct available to those who are privileged and powerful—or to those temporarily allied with the privileged and powerful. The same tendency repeats itself when students ally themselves with Shylock and refuse to see that he can be both sinned against and sinning, and that Antonio can be a bigot who nonetheless does not deserve to die.

The farcical nature of justice represented in the courtroom is then repeated when the characters return to Belmont in the last act of the play. Here is where they negotiate the issue of the rings. After demanding the rings from Bassanio and Gratiano and being told that they had given them in gratitude to "Balthazar" and his "clerk," Portia and her maid claim to have received them back from the lawyer and his assistant when they "lay with" them. Before the situation escalates, however, all is revealed—namely, that Portia and Nerissa were disguised as Balthazar and his assistant and thus that Bassanio and Gratiano gave their rings to them, the original owners.

We are back where we began in a society where women are chaste and subordinate, the Jew is uninflectedly villainous and must be forced to convert, and the gay man is relegated to the sidelines, erased from view. It is a decidedly awkward and unsatisfying conclusion after what has transpired. It papers over the disruptive insights and feelings aroused in the process of returning. Given Shakespeare's restless, empathetic imagination, it seems inevitable that he would revisit the themes and character issues raised in this play and would give them more elaborated treatment in his subsequent work.

5

As You Like It

Gender

Many male writers have created female characters without being empathetic toward women. One could even argue that the majority of great male writers in the Anglo-American tradition have given their female characters attributes that reinforce, even amplify, misogynistic stereotypes. I would cite Spenser, Milton, Pope, Fielding, Hemingway, Nabokov, Roth, and Updike as a quick sampling.

But Shakespeare was an exception. He was preternaturally open to new facets of experience, including new ways of understanding oneself. And as an actor as well as a playwright at a time when men performed women's roles, he must have been led to think more deeply about what it meant to inhabit the female position, not just to write about it for the purpose of forwarding an idea or furthering a plot.

To play a woman is to imagine *being* a woman, leading, in turn, to the creation of works that also explore what it must feel like for a woman to play a man—and beyond that, to consider if there is a difference between *playing* and *being*. This seems to me precisely what happens in the cross-dressing comedies, natural extensions of Shakespeare's tendency to sketch a situation and then, once it is imagined, feel driven to elaborate it.

Two Gentlemen of Verona, The Merchant of Venice, As You Like It, Twelfth Night, and *Cymbeline* all involve female characters spending an extended period of time posing as men. *Two Gentlemen of Verona,* among Shakespeare's first plays, introduces cross-dressing, while *Cymbeline,* said by some to be a kind of parody by Shakespeare of some of his then-familiar themes, is concerned, as are all his late Romances, with the nature of mortality and the extension of life into future generations. In neither play does it seem to me that Shakespeare is interested in exploring gender in any consistent or profound way.

The Merchant of Venice is far more important in this regard. The second of Shakespeare's three cross-dressing comedies, this play, as I have noted, explores the woman's position as both outsider and insider—both victim and punisher—within two kinds of society: the workaday commercial world of Venice and the more exotic, romantic world of Belmont. Both are governed by patriarchal law: one by the formal law of commerce, the other by the capricious law of Portia's late father. In both, Portia is able to navigate and achieve her ends but in each case through trickery. The play is labeled a comedy, though much of its overall tone is dark, and its ending contains decidedly tragic elements.

Twelfth Night, which follows *As You Like It* directly, seems to have other concerns in mind. The twin brother and sister in this play are substitutable for each other. Gender has receded as a central preoccupation in favor of an exploration of emotional excess and the lengths needed to subdue such feeling and control its repercussions. It is not that Shakespeare ceases to be interested in gender but that he now incorporates empathy for the gendered Other more naturally into his plays.

But in *As You Like It,* written a few years after *The Merchant of Venice* and around the same time as *Twelfth Night,* Shakespeare not only uses cross-dressing to further the plot, he uses it to interrogate the meanings and implications of gender roles. He makes us *feel* for both men and women who must operate within the constraints of "doublet and hose" and "petticoat." In this respect, it is a pivotal play in Shakespeare's evolving empathetic imagination.

As You Like It is a festive comedy, and there is little to dim its lightness and brightness. In keeping with its tone, its use of cross-dressing seems directed at different or at least more expansive ends than that of *The Merchant of Venice.* Whereas *Merchant* seems intent on playing marginal characters off against one another, *As You Like* is involved with exploring gender more broadly, finding in both male and female roles aspects of vulnerability that can lead to greater acceptance and equality between the sexes. In the end, the play is philosophical about how society is organized and how men and women behave and interact with each other. It pushes beyond these themes to explore the way gender roles are themselves "constructed." Its sense of empathy for the gendered position—and the pains and difficulties that accompany it on both sides—is at the heart of its comic warmth.

Celia and Rosalind are cousins and devoted friends. Celia's father, Duke Frederick, has usurped the throne from his older brother Duke Senior (Rosalind's father and Celia's uncle) and sent him into exile. Duke Frederick soon wants to banish niece Rosalind, too. But Celia will not allow her cousin to leave the court without her and insists on their fleeing together to the Forest of Arden, where Duke Senior is leading a rustic life with his banished courtiers.

The decision by Celia and Rosalind to run off together involves their also deciding to disguise themselves as brother and sister. Rosalind takes the name Ganymede, who was Jove's page and erstwhile lover; Celia takes the name Aliena. The relationship between Celia and Rosalind encourages us to consider the implications of both their new presentation as brother and sister and their previous relationship as devoted cousins and friends

> We still have slept together,
> Rose at an instant, learned, played, eat together,
> And wheresoe'er we went, like Juno's swans,
> Still we went coupled and inseparable. (1.3.65–68)

My students in recent years have been fascinated by the relationship between Rosalind and Celia. They now take the possibility of a lesbian relationship between these women seriously where once they might have snickered at the thought and, before that, never considered it at all. This says something about how societal attitudes on what constitutes a couple have changed as well as how much more open, relaxed, and imaginative the atmosphere of my classroom has become.

I believe that Shakespeare imagined everything that we can imagine today, and that Celia and Rosalind's relationship is meant to be provocative and confusing from the outset. That they do not quite fit into clear categories as daughters, cousins, pretend-siblings, or conventional women in a royal court seems to be the point. For the play goes on to make us ponder the concept of identity—of how our gender, our dress, even our stature, and our emotional responsiveness define us.

In what is, to my mind, the most important and diverting aspect of the play, Rosalind, disguised as Ganymede, interacts with Orlando (the youngest son of a deceased nobleman), who has also fled to the forest. They had previously met at court in act 1 and fallen in love at first sight. Now Rosalind, in disguise and presumably unrecognizable to Orlando, insists that he "practice" his courtship and pretend that "he," Ganymede, is Orlando's beloved Rosalind. The overlaying of the apparently real person with the person acting the part, not to mention the actor beneath it all (played by a boy in Shakespeare's day), raises the question of whether we play at being ourselves and what that says about who we "really" are.

Part of the point of the playacting, as Rosalind-disguised-as-Ganymede explains to Orlando, is to teach him about women's capricious ways and to "cure" him of love. She maligns her sex in the guise of a woman playing a man playing a woman: "O, that woman that cannot make her fault her husband's occasion, let her never nurse her child herself for she will breed it like a fool" (4.1.154–156). But her playacting is in reality, given her love for Orlando, a *lesson* in courtship. It is intended to teach him how to spar on a variety of topics and how to hold to his position in the face of an opponent. If women are critiqued in the process, men are implicitly critiqued for making women what they are through negligence, infidelity, and cruelty.

The mutuality of abuse is the underlying motif of the courtship and the reason why, presumably, it is needed: "men are April when they woo, December when they wed; maids are May when they are maids, but the sky changes when they are wives" (4.1.129–132). The implication is that each sex takes advantage of the other, men and women both putting on a front until they have secured what they want. Unlike the Jew in *The Merchant of Venice*, who is *made* into an abuser by having suffered longstanding abuse, here the blame seems more symmetrically shared. Although women in other Shakespeare plays—*The Taming of the Shrew, Much Ado About Nothing,* and *Othello,* for example—will be placed explicitly in the victim position, in *As*

You Like It, Rosalind and Celia have more independence and agency (albeit with Rosalind disguised, for most of the play, as a man).

The conceit of cross-dressing, which Shakespeare used so provocatively in *The Merchant of Venice* but kept narrowly confined within the demands of a particular end (saving Antonio from having to deliver up his pound of flesh), has become a larger, looser element in this play—more of a philosophical diversion than a plot point. As such, it lends itself to a kind of speculation that the other play only begins to suggest. Students reading *As You Like It* constantly switch their loyalties. Orlando's willingness to playact with the disguised Rosalind seems at once perverse and delightful. Is it, in fact, a kind of disloyalty to his original love, or is it a tribute to that loyalty? Is Rosalind's teasing of Orlando a test or a form of emasculation and even abuse? Is she exposing how women retaliate against men for making them subordinate and subservient, or is she critiquing the fickleness and duplicity of the female nature? All these possibilities are in play during their scenes together.

Rosalind-as-Ganymede's glib, rather brutal and cynical schooling of Orlando in the capriciousness of women's ways is always followed, when she is alone with Celia, by distraught concern for his attentiveness. Ganymede is callous with Orlando (and with two other lovelorn characters, Phoebe and Sylvius, as well), but Rosalind is vulnerable and needy with her cousin. Reason and emotion oscillate: Ganymede-alternating-with-Rosalind is by turns harsh and tender, sarcastic and sincere. Is the latter the real self or is it another performance? Significantly, we never see Rosalind or Rosalind-as-Ganymede outside of her relationships. In neither role does she have a soliloquy from which we can gain access to her inner thoughts.

The crisis point in the situation occurs when Rosalind-as-Ganymede learns that Orlando has been wounded saving his brother Oliver from a lion. She faints, thereby destroying the coherence of the character in front of Oliver, who assumes he is dealing with a man—and men, in the lexicon that has been set up here, do not faint: "I pray you tell your brother how well I counterfeited" (4.3.164–165), Rosalind-as-Ganymede begs. The scene wonderfully brings home the respective assumptions ascribed to the male and female roles, and poignantly makes clear how deprived men are of an outlet for powerful feeling. Indeed, this scene demonstrates what *As You Like It* seems concerned with throughout as a function of its gender-bending antics: it encourages us to imagine the limitations attached to the gendered role that we do not inhabit and to empathize with those who must suffer under these limitations, whether men or women.

Students often say that Rosalind-as-Ganymede is a proto-example of a gender-fluid individual, someone who requires a "they" pronoun. But that plurality, while it opens the character to more possibilities and meanings, also diffuses our ability to focus what we feel and think.

This is rectified in the last scene of the play when "Ganymede" is transformed back into Rosalind. (The character announces that this will be done by magic, but we know that it will simply mean removing a disguise.) Here, finally, the oscillation ceases. Rosalind is revealed as the daughter of Duke Senior and the soon-to-be wife of Orlando. Yet in the epilogue, Shakespeare has the boy actor playing Rosalind appear out of costume and address the audience in his male identity: "If I were a woman, I would kiss as many of you as had beards that pleased me, complexions that liked me, and breaths that I defied not" (ll. 15–17). Rosalind's return to a singular female identity is thus undercut by this additional shedding of costume. The "reveal" is a plea to open ourselves to possibility in how we see—and feel about—others. We are being encouraged to "kiss" those who appeal to us, whether bearded or not, whatever their "complexions"—an idea that will be pointedly returned to in *Othello*.

If the play opens us to others, it also opens us to ourselves. In the return of Rosalind to a seemingly singular identity—which the epilogue reminds us is not really singular—we are led to think about what lies beneath our more workaday role-playing in the world: perhaps some primal character, some Other. To what extent are we "playing" ourselves, and if so, what is real and what is false in our performance? If we can begin to think of the self as a performance, we can begin to think about performing different kinds of selves and, hence, becoming more tolerant and open to difference in general.

The empathy we are encouraged to feel toward gender difference and gender fluidity associated with Rosalind takes us back to consider the heroine in *The Merchant of Venice*. In the last scene of that play, Portia, having shed her male disguise and returned to Belmont, castigates Bassanio for giving away her ring—the ring that she herself took from him in her disguise as Balthazar as a token of Bassanio's gratitude for Balthazar's saving Antonio's life. She then shows him the ring, giving rise to his suspicion that she slept with the man to whom he gave it. This is a prefiguration, one could say, of the kind of mock disloyalty that occurs between Orlando and Rosalind in *As You Like It*, in which the male character is, in a sense, unfaithful to a woman with a man who turns out to be the woman herself.

The circuit of the ring in *The Merchant of Venice*—from Portia to Bassanio and back to her again—adds yet another dimension to the situation. My students have suggested that the return of the ring to its original owner can be understood to reflect the marriage of Portia to herself. This may seem eccentric, but in fact it is consistent with contemporary notions of self-empowerment and self-care. There is actually a term, *sologamy,* coined in 2017, for a marriage to oneself. But for all its contemporaneity, the idea also seems one that would have occurred to Shakespeare, given his extraordinarily fertile and prescient imagination. While it is true, as I have noted, that his greatest characters exist in relationships, there is also an acute awareness that some relationships can be toxic and distort the self. Keeping an aspect of that self apart and protected can be useful, particularly for those in vulnerable positions. All the cross-dressing heroines, if not all the heroines in Shakespeare, are profoundly vulnerable.

The symbolism of the rings can also be understood in the context of gender conflation—of the incorporation of male into female and female into male: the collapsing of a shifting, flux-like identity into a more stable self that seems singular on the surface but contains the depth of Otherness beneath (what Freud would refer to as the unconscious or id). This idea of the self anticipates a nonbinary concept of identity that has become part of our current understanding of gender. At the same time, the play returns to the status quo, repressing what might challenge a conventionally gendered self. This, as my students will admit, is a useful if disappointing way to contain Otherness in the world as it existed at that time.[1]

Let me end with the observation that some students also put forward: what might have been a practical way to resolve confused gender identity in Shakespeare's day may no longer be so in our own. Now a fluid, nonbinary self may be *more* fitted than a static, binary one to a landscape dominated by competing and contradictory messages. In short, where Shakespeare would have seen disorder, even chaos, we are likely to see diversity and possibility. In such a context, the concept of identity has evolved accordingly.

This is an idea the playwright may have contemplated in his 1606 tragedy *Antony and Cleopatra.* Cleopatra's changeableness is central to her identity, rather than a mere disguise. Antony's fascination with her is a function of her "infinite variety." He, for his part, is (or becomes—as he engages with her) "allied" with her way of being. Her variety, one could say, incites his. As I shall discuss below, these characters lead us to an empathetic perspective that redefines the heroic life in new, more compassionate terms.

6

Hamlet

Self

Hamlet is a prince whose uncle has killed his father and assumed the throne, and whose mother has blithely married her husband's murderer. The action takes place in the remote state of Denmark, and a ghost makes an appearance in the first scene. It is hard to think of a situation more outside the ken of the playwright or, for that matter, of audience and readers. Neither he nor many of us has been to Denmark, led the life of a prince, or suffered the murder of our father, a king. Most of us have not seen a ghost. Yet the play is the most popular in Shakespeare's canon, despite being his longest, because we empathize with its protagonist not as an Other but as a version of ourselves. We feel for Hamlet because we feel our own predicament in his, despite its being so seemingly different from our own.

In the two dozen or so times that I have taught *Hamlet,* I have asked myself and my students, Where does this character come from? How could Shakespeare have conceived of a personality that is at once enormously contradictory and vibrantly real and capable of eliciting both our identification and our empathy?

It is possible to see Richard II and Henry V growing out of the truncated moral vision of Richard III. And to see Othello and even Lear as extrapolations from the extraordinary speech in *The Merchant of Venice* in which the vilified Jew expounds on his humanity and explains his villainy. We can see how female characters as different as Rosalind, Emilia (Iago's wife in *Othello*), and Cleopatra grew out of the fact that boys played girls in Shakespeare's day and, hence, encouraged him to indulge in imaginative role-playing.

But Hamlet? I suggested earlier that Hal, later Henry V, may have set Shakespeare's imagination moving in the direction of a divided self, and that the cross-dressing comedies reinforced this concept. Still, the division of the private and public man in Henry V, and of the male and female role-playing of Rosalind-as-Ganymede, hardly prepares us for Hamlet's complex, existentially fraught condition. No previous character has his dramatic shifts in mood and behavior: his flippant wit and wordplay, his passionate excoriation of others alternating with tenderness and sorrow, his cold-blooded decision to send his former friends to their deaths, and his profound ruminations on suicide. It all somehow coheres. Students I have taught from the beginning of my career through to the present have identified with Hamlet, have found him real, poignant, and comprehensible without being able to say exactly why. How, then, was Shakespeare able to combine so many disparate elements to create a character to whom people can viscerally relate hundreds of years later?

To begin to answer this question, I want to consider why the play begins as it does. Beginnings are important to Shakespeare— think of Gloucester's powerful opening soliloquy on his disability, Antonio's opening announcement of his mysterious depression, and Romeo's initial pining after Rosaline before he encounters Juliet. Each of these passages is not really important to the plot but enormously important in introducing something essential about a character integral to the play's action. So why does Shakespeare open *Hamlet* by having Hamlet's best and most rational friend, Horatio, encounter Hamlet's father's ghost before he does?

> MARCELLUS: Is it not like the king?
> HORATIO: As thou art to thyself.
>   Such was the very armour he had on
>   When he th'ambitious Norway combated;
>   So frowned he once, when in an angry parle
>   He smote the sledded Polacks on the ice.
>   'Tis strange. (1.1.58–64)

Marcellus and Horatio, as well as another watchman, Bernardo, have been assigned to stand guard at night for enemies of their country (specifically, for the young Fortinbras, Prince of Norway, the character who will, with Horatio, be the last man standing at the end of the play). But the watchmen encounter not an enemy from outside their borders in this first scene but an armed ghost of their former king, who will later warn Hamlet of an enemy from within. In act 3, that enemy is confirmed with Claudius's soliloquy, in which he confesses that he has killed his brother in order to take possession of his throne and his queen.

With the premise of a crime established, the result might have been the kind of revenge narrative popular at the time—the sort of thing that contemporaries like Thomas Kyd or Francis Beaumont and John Fletcher (who may have collaborated with Shakespeare on other plays) might have produced.

But Shakespeare does not choose to follow this route. The crime is there, made evident to us from an early point in the story, but even before Hamlet suspects King Claudius, he is shown to be suffering for reasons that have nothing to do with regicide and that continue to plague him after he learns his father has been murdered by his uncle. Why, for example, does the "To be or not to be" speech—Hamlet's anguished contemplation of the pros and cons of suicide—occur not before he sees the ghost of his father but after? Why, when he finally has a clear-cut reason to seek justice, is he led to think about killing himself?

> To die, to sleep—
> No more; and by a sleep to say we end
> The heart-ache and the thousand natural shocks
> That flesh is heir to—'tis a consummation
> Devoutly to be wished. To die, to sleep—
> To sleep, perchance to dream. Ay, there's the rub,
> For in that sleep of death what dreams may come,
> When we have shuffled off this mortal coil,
> Must give us pause. (3.1.60–68)

His misery, as expressed in this mix of desire for and fear of death, seems connected to something other and even more emotionally debilitating than his outrage at his mother's marriage and the criminal behavior of his uncle.

Here is where Freud stepped in to argue that the character's real problem lay with an unresolved Oedipus complex: Hamlet's father's death and his mother's remarriage are at the source of his problem. In this psychoanalytic interpretation, the revenge plot is a cover for an oedipal struggle. But if Hamlet's misery reflects his personal oedipal issues, why do other characters—Bernardo, Marcellus, and especially the supremely rational Horatio—also see the ghost of Hamlet's father? Indeed, they see it before Hamlet himself does, making it impossible to argue, as one might be inclined, that Hamlet has incited a mass delusion in his friends.

Other critics of the play simply ignore the issue of when and why Hamlet's suffering begins and interpret him as a character whose excessive rumination impedes his ability to act. They concentrate on a single issue: faced with a clear directive from the ghost of his father, he delays and philosophizes. But this seems wrong, too. The one direct statement Hamlet makes about being indecisive occurs as he is contemplating suicide:

> Thus conscience does make cowards of us all,
> And thus the native hue of resolution
> Is sicklied o'er with the pale cast of thought,
> And enterprises of great pitch and moment
> With this regard their currents turn awry
> And lose the name of action. (3.1.83–88)

The assumption that Hamlet here moves from indecisiveness about suicide to indecisiveness about other things deserves examination. It is glossed over, as though there is no dissonance between the two kinds of action. Indeed, while Hamlet is certainly a thinker—and one who here is seriously torn on the subject of suicide—he is also a man who proceeds to act decisively in other contexts: stabbing the hidden Polonius without a second's hesitation, arranging for Rosencrantz and Guildenstern's deaths, negotiating effectively with pirates, dueling with Laertes. The problem is not that Hamlet cannot act; it is that he cannot act in particular circumstances—that is, those in which his father's ghost directs him to act.

What puts these elements into context is Hamlet's relationship to kingship. Why hasn't he inherited the throne?[1] I have already discussed how in the Henriad the law of primogeniture originally functioned to produce orderly succession, and the dire consequences that result when it is breached. Does Shakespeare want us to ignore the orderly law of inheritance because the play is set in Denmark and not England? Or is Hamlet's failure to be crowned king another instance of something "rotten" about the state of his nation? But if so, why is no mention made of this lapse in succession until the last scene of the play, when Hamlet, as he prepares to duel with Laertes, refers to Claudius as having "killed my king, and whored my mother, / Popped in between th'election and my hopes" (5.2.64–65)?

I propose that Hamlet's right to the throne is not addressed in the play until the moment when he is prepared to die because it does not matter to him. His focus is backward rather than forward—toward the past rather than toward the present and future. He remains tethered to an idealized, romanticized view of his parents. "Must I remember? why she would hang on him / As if increase of appetite had grown / By what it fed on" (1.2.143–145), he laments in his first soliloquy, remembering his mother's devotion to his father. He does not conceive of himself as the father of his country or of anyone else ("Get thee to a nunnery—why wouldst thou be a / breeder of sinners?" [3.1.120–121]), he explodes at Ophelia), but as a son who has lost not his birthright so much as the idyll of his childhood: "Must I remember?"

Children begin by believing in a united parental unit, devoted to their well-being, and they want to continue to believe in this idealized image of comfort and safety even as time and experience prove it wrong. Hamlet is deeply attached to this idealized image, which circumstances have abruptly and brutally shattered. When he mistakenly stabs Polonius, he cannot concentrate on what he has done—murdered an innocent man—but remains fixated on his father's perfection. He holds up the pictures of father and uncle to his mother:

> Look here upon this picture, and on this,
> The counterfeit presentment of two brothers.

He then proceeds to describe his father in absurdly idealized terms:

> See what a grace was seated on this brow;
> Hyperion's curls, the front of Jove himself,
> An eye like Mars, to threaten and command;
> A station like the herald Mercury,
> New-lighted on a heaven-kissing hill. (3.4.53–59)

We find support for this reading of Hamlet's regressive perspective at the beginning of act 5 when he recalls an idyll of youth with the jester Yorick, now reduced to a skull that he recovers from a turned-over grave. Soon after, he jumps into Ophelia's newly dug grave, where he boasts of his devotion to her and challenges her brother, Laertes, to a duel. Laertes was a companion from childhood, and both the ranting in the open grave and the decision to duel seem to reflect childlike competitiveness.

These backward-turning images and impulses seem key to understanding Hamlet's character. Shakespeare has managed, through the various elements in the plot, to represent a man who suffers in exaggerated form the existential crisis we all face at some point—of losing our parents through their literal death or, more often, through their change in our eyes as we see them as flawed and vulnerable human beings. This is what Hamlet suffers, and what the intervention of his father's ghost brings to a crisis by placing him in a position of filial duty. Hamlet knows he should avenge his father, but having his father tell him to do so obliterates his independent judgment and choice in action. That Claudius killed his father is therefore of less importance to the fraught nature of Hamlet's position than that his father has come back, armed in all his former authority, to demand that he do something about it.

This adds meaning to the fact that the ghost is seen first by others before being seen by Hamlet. Hamlet Sr.'s valor and authority are immediately recognized by Horatio and Bernardo, which means that his son cannot pretend that he is acting on his own. His father is still present to his friends as well as to himself as the de facto king, while the literal king, Claudius, holds the reins of power for everyone else (including Hamlet's false friends Rosencrantz and Guildenstern). Hamlet's capacity for independent judgment and authority is thus entirely usurped by both the new stepfather and the return of the real father. By the same token, seeing his father's ghost reawakens the childhood idyll he imagines existed and still yearns for but that his mother has either betrayed or, worse, proven false by her ability to shift her allegiance so easily to his father's brother.

When my students discuss this play, Hamlet's position strikes a deeply resonant note. Many of them are very close to their parents—they speak to them on the phone every day (or more). I've had students tell me without embarrassment that their parents are their best friends, that they rely on them to allay their anxiety before an exam or before a date, and to assuage their hurt when these things go badly. At the same time, they want desperately to "be their own person" and show initiative (one of the most popular majors right now at my and many other universities is "entrepreneurship"). When we discuss *Hamlet,* the contradiction between familial loyalty and self-empowerment emerges clearly. Ideas that were raised (and that I referenced) in discussions of *Richard II*—where students tended to align simply with one or the other of these values—become more complicated. *Hamlet* brings to the surface the fact that what we may believe in one context may differ radically in another.

One could also say that Shakespeare has taken the paradigm that structured the plot of *Richard II*—an old world usurped by a new one—and placed it into the mind of a single, acutely sensitive individual. Hamlet exists in a kind of limbo, poised between the old world of childhood and the new world of independent adulthood. This is both his unique dilemma and one that all of us share, to some extent, as we grow older. For we always remain our parents' children at the same time that we struggle to replace the dependent, pliant creatures we once were with stronger, more well-defined selves. Freud sexualized this struggle, but though sexuality is certainly at issue in the play, the deeper issue is one of judgment and will. What must we give up in order to become masters of our own destiny—indeed, how can we become masters when the past holds a grip on us that can seem impossible to escape?

This question directs the ending of the play. Hamlet's "readiness" for death characterizes his approach to the duel with Laertes: "If it be now, 'tis not to come; if it be not to come, it will be now; if it be not now, yet it will come—the readiness is all" (5.2.204–206). Hamlet's readiness becomes a way to solve the double bind of his position: to do what his dead father bids him to do while not explicitly succumbing to that directive. The resolution entails his death, which he can rationalize as a chosen course, not a dictated one.

To be "ready" for death is to be, in the largest sense, at ease with one's mortality—to have acquired the most comprehensive, philosophical perspective possible. As represented in the play, however, we are made to see that we can attain this perspective only when other alternatives are blocked. Hamlet, we could argue, perhaps like us all, is cornered into insight. This is characteristic of what I would call Shakespeare's skeptical humanism: he sees the complex foundation of even the most seemingly elevated positions. We get to them through circuitous, often dubious, routes.

We could say that the route Hamlet takes ultimately involves navigating between two extremes. One extreme is represented by Horatio, whom Hamlet extols in act 3 as the epitome of steadfast loyalty. Their friendship, begun presumably in childhood, has remained unchanged:

> Since my dear soul was mistress of her choice,
> And could of men distinguish her election,
> Sh'ath sealed thee for herself, for thou hast been
> As one in suffering all that suffers nothing,
> A man that Fortune's buffets and rewards
> Hast tane with equal thanks. And blest are those
> Whose blood and judgement are so well commeddled
> That they are not a pipe for Fortune's finger
> To sound what stop she please. Give me that man
> That is not passion's slave, and I will wear him
> In my heart's core, ay in my heart of heart,
> As I do thee. (3.2.58–69)

The other extreme is represented by Claudius. He shows a ruthless embrace of the fact that things change, time marches on, and we must look forward, not back. His speech to Hamlet in act 1, purely self-serving in context, is, when taken by itself, enormously pragmatic and, in its way, wise:

> 'Tis sweet and commendable in your nature Hamlet,
> To give these mourning duties to your father;
> But you must know, your father lost a father,
> That father lost, lost his, and the survivor bound
> In filial obligation for some term
> To do obsequious sorrow; but to persever
> In obstinate condolement is a course
> Of impious stubbornness, 'tis unmanly grief,

It shows a will most incorrect to heaven,
A heart unfortified, a mind impatient,
An understanding simple and unschooled.
For what we know must be, and is as common
As any the most vulgar thing to sense,
Why should we in our peevish opposition
Take it to heart? Fie, 'tis a fault to heaven,
A fault against the dead, a fault to nature,
To reason most absurd, whose common theme
Is death of fathers, and who still hath cried,
From the first corse till he that died today,
"This must be so." (1.2.87–106)

Horatio and Claudius each represents a position with a certain appeal: unchanging devotion on the one hand, pragmatic acceptance of what we are dealt—or can make happen—on the other. But these are theoretical positions only. Each is a foil to Hamlet, who alone embodies the fully human character, torn between nostalgia for the safety and simplicity of the past and the need to define himself and grow in the present.

If we are thinking and feeling people, we struggle with these opposing impulses of stasis and change, of a devotion to the past and a drive toward the future, until the push and pull ends and we die. Hamlet, for all his special attributes and circumstances, mirrors our struggle. This is why he remains, of all Shakespeare's characters, the one who evokes both our identification and our empathy. We feel for him because we feel for ourselves.

7

Othello

Race and Class

*O*thello seems to me profoundly dependent on the existence of *The Merchant of Venice.* I am convinced that Shakespeare would not have been drawn to the story, "Un Capitano Moro" (1565) by Giraldi Cinthio, on which *Othello* is based had he not begun to contemplate the issues raised in that earlier play.

Two passages from *Merchant* are key to understanding this evolution: one is a single sentence stated in passing by the heroine, the other a major speech given by the villain. Both seem crucial in setting the playwright's imagination moving in a particular direction.

Let all of his complexion choose me so. (2.7.79)

Early in the play, Portia is residing at her bucolic estate, Belmont, entertaining suitors who must choose one of the three caskets that her father, before he died, stipulated be presented to any man who wished to become her husband. Each of these caskets—made of gold, silver, and lead—is inscribed with a riddle, and the man who deciphers the riddle of the correct casket will win her hand. In a rather transparent irony, the lead casket, which is inscribed, "Who chooseth me, must give and hazard all he hath" (2.7.9), is the right one and the one that Bassanio, with hints from Portia, chooses.

But before Bassanio makes his way to Belmont, the first suitor to arrive is the Prince of Morocco, who picks the gold casket with the inscription "Who chooseth me, shall get as much as he deserves" (2.7.23). This is the wrong casket, as the inscription on a skull inside chides: "All that glisters is not gold" (2.7.65).

The prince who makes this first, wrong choice is identified as a black man. He presents himself (much as Othello will do in the later play) as aware of the prejudice Portia may have against his skin color:

> Mislike me not for my complexion,
> . . .
> I tell thee, lady, this aspect of mine
> Hath feared the valiant; by my love I swear
> The best-regarded virgins of our clime
> Have loved it too. I would not change this hue
> Except to steal your thoughts, my gentle queen. (2.1.1,
> 8–12)

Portia assures the Prince that she is "not solely led / By nice direction of a maiden's eyes" (2.1.13–14), an indirect denigration of his skin color. Besides, she has no choice but to follow her father's orders (much like Hamlet here—though both, it might be noted, find ways to exercise their will in the face of paternal directives). But Portia *is* put off by the Prince's blackness, judging by her relief when he chooses wrongly: "Let all of his complexion choose me so," she says in an aside. This line would probably not have bothered his largely white audience at the time and, I would suggest, did not bother mostly white audiences up through the recent past.

And yet as the plot unfolds and Shylock's mix of humanity and villainy becomes evident, Portia's statement about the Prince's complexion may have stayed with Shakespeare and made him consider its larger implications. That throwaway line might have taken on more weight in the face of Shylock's famous speech, which constitutes, to my mind, the second major instigation for the creation of Othello.

> Hath not a Jew eyes? Hath not a Jew hands, organs, dimensions, senses, affections, passions? Fed with the same food, hurt with the same weapons, subject to the same diseases, healed by the same means, warmed and cooled by the same winter and summer as a Christian is? If you prick us, do we not bleed? . . . If a Jew wrong a Christian, what is his humility? Revenge. If a Christian wrong a Jew, what should his sufferance be by Christian example? Why, revenge! The villainy you teach me, I will execute, and it shall go hard but I will better the instruction. (3.1.50–62)

This powerful speech is actually recycled in amended form in *Othello,* but here it is given to the secondary female character, Emilia, Iago's wife, as she speaks to her mistress Desdemona (Othello's wife). Emilia first acknowledges women's mistreatment by men, then goes on:

> Yet have we some revenge. Let husbands know
> Their wives have sense like them: they see, and smell,
> And have their palates both for sweet and sour

As husbands have. What is it that they do
When they change us for others? Is it sport?
I think it is. And doth affection breed it?
I think it doth. Is't frailty that thus errs?
It is so too. And have not we affections,
Desires for sport, and frailty, as men have?
Then let them use us well; else let them know
The ills we do, their ills instruct us so. (4.3.90–100)

The parallels to Shylock's speech are obvious, though the poetry is more assimilated to blank verse than Shylock's freer
but no less eloquent expression. These lines are also put in the
mouth of a woman who will, in compliance with her husband's
wishes, become an accessory to Iago's plot (how knowingly is
hard to say, though she certainly regrets the result and ends up
paying with her life).

In *Othello*, Shakespeare takes the Other and places him at
the center of the narrative. This character now has heroic qualities
and is positioned to elicit sympathy as well as empathy—unlike
Shylock, who earns empathy incidentally and only if we are attentive. Othello is a Christian convert and a great general, indis-
pensable to the Venetian state and attractive enough to win the
hand of the rich and beautiful Desdemona. But his blackness
from the beginning sounds a dissonant note with the other characters. Iago hates Othello for having denied him the promotion
he thinks he deserves, giving it instead to the younger, inexperi-
enced Cassio; but he also makes racist comments in the process
of lamenting the injustice. He yells out to Brabantio, Desdemona's
father, as part of his effort to destroy Othello, "Even now, now,
very now, an old black ram / Is tupping your white ewe," and in
an attempt to play further on Brabantio's race prejudice: "You'll
have your daughter covered with a Barbary horse, you'll have
your nephews neigh to you" (1.1.89–90, 111–113).

Brabantio, for his part, is responsive to these kinds of taunts. He emphatically opposes Othello as a son-in-law because Othello is black. He laments that his daughter has "run from her guardage to the sooty bosom / Of such a thing as thou" (1.2.70–71).

Most important—and disturbing—Othello himself is acutely conscious of and uncomfortable in his Otherness. His sense of not belonging becomes the means by which Iago convinces him of his wife's infidelity. Iago presents his argument to Othello under the guise of honest friendship but with the devious aim of playing on Othello's insecurity as a black man in a white society:

> Ay, there's the point: as, to be bold with you,
> Not to affect many proposèd matches
> Of her own clime, complexion, and degree,
> Whereto we see in all things nature tends—
> Foh! one may smell, in such, a will most rank,
> Foul disproportion, thoughts unnatural. (3.3.230–235)

That Othello can accept this argument—that Desdemona's decision to marry him was "unnatural"—reflects what my students refer to as his abysmally low self-esteem.

But the injustice leveled against Othello as an Other is not the only example of injustice in this play. Injustice in one form or another is everywhere, and even the most egregious villains— the Iagos of the world—can suffer it and, if we pay attention, evoke our empathy.

Othello, who invests enormous confidence in Iago's honesty and loyalty, fails to see that his "ancient" (ensign) is resentful at having been passed over for promotion to his lieutenant. He is as blind to Iago's ambition as Desdemona's father is blind to the possibility that Othello might fall in love with (and be loved by) his daughter. In both cases, the physical appearance of the individual—Iago's unpolished demeanor in the eyes of Othello, Othello's blackness in the eyes of Brabantio—makes him invisible in certain respects. Othello can depend on Iago's judgment and counsel but cannot imagine him as a lieutenant; Brabantio can entertain Othello in his home but cannot imagine him as a son-in-law. What does this tell us about what we may be blind to, what prejudices of which we are not aware may be causing us to dismiss or wound others, even those close to us, or to engage in practices that are cruel without our realizing it? It is an exercise that I pose to my class whenever I teach this play, and which we try to answer together.[1]

Iago is able to incite paranoia in Othello because Othello sees himself as Other, as less worthy of being loved than a person of another complexion. He assumes that Desdemona chose him *despite* his blackness. This becomes the lever that Iago uses to create paranoia and jealousy. Why wouldn't Desdemona be unfaithful, given how "unnatural" it was for her to have fallen in love with Othello in the first place? Why would she not choose to love Cassio, who is white and shares her upbringing and background?

What supports this argument is that Othello promoted Cassio for precisely the reason that, according to Iago, Desdemona would "naturally" choose him as her lover—because he fits the appearance of what is expected. Iago understands this early on when he bitterly decries Othello's choice of lieutenant:

> One Michael Cassio, a Florentine,
> A fellow almost damned in a fair wife,
> That never set a squadron in the field,
> Nor the devision of a battle knows
> More than a spinster, unless the bookish theoric,
> Wherein the togèd consuls can propose

As masterly as he. Mere prattle without practice
Is all his soldiership. (1.1.20–27)

Othello and Iago are similar in having both been perceived
as lesser, though each is initially in a different position with
respect to a marginal group. Othello, by exhibiting extraordinary merit as a military leader, has been able to elevate himself
above other black men in white Venetian society. Iago has not
shown such talent or had such luck, and he has remained in the
lesser position associated with his class. Othello seems initially content with what he has achieved. Iago is consumed with
bitterness and resentment at having been passed over.

Yet as different as they seem in their initial positioning,
these characters end up in much the same place: Othello's murder of Desdemona mirrors Iago's destruction of Othello. Both
have been driven to villainy by a wound to their humanity. Both
reflect the logic, albeit followed through in different ways, that
drove the psychologically scarred Shylock.

It is indeed worth noting how much *Othello* has taken the
outline of *The Merchant of Venice* and extrapolated it to deal
with race and gender with greater depth and complexity. The
new addition here is class, and this is something that continues
to be overlooked by many critics when dealing with the play.

I tend to think that Shakespeare was attuned to the class
issue that drives Iago's resentment, given his own "mixed"
background. His mother's family came from the minor gentry
(they owned a small amount of land), and his father was in trade
(tradesmen were looked down upon by members of the British
land-owning class up through the twentieth century). The
tensions that may have resulted from this disparity and from
related challenges facing Shakespeare's father, who was reportedly imprisoned for not paying his debts, would have registered
on an observant and sensitive child. Contributing to his sense

of class consciousness was the fact that Shakespeare lacked the kind of formal education expected of an important writer (he had "small Latin and less Greek," wrote his fellow playwright Ben Jonson). I would add that class prejudice on the part of future generations is what has fueled the suspicion that some-one else wrote the plays. How, the reasoning goes, could a man with such limited social and educational opportunities have written such great work? Yet the question gets things backward: Shakespeare's gifts derive from his existing *outside* conven-tional categories—in his ability to imagine how others, different from the educated elite of his society, might feel and act.

My speculation regarding the prejudices associated with lower-class status in Shakespeare's day—and still operating in our own—can be applied to the character of Iago. The lack of empathy that audiences and readers have felt and still feel for Iago strikes me as an exaggerated version of the lack of empathy that long surrounded Shylock before the latter's ethnic identity began to gain him a following. Iago has no speech on a par with Shylock's "hath not a Jew eyes," but he does explain his sense of injured merit early in the play:

> Three great ones of the city,
> In personal suit to make me his lieutenant,
> Off-capp'd to him; and, by the faith of man,
> I know my price, I am worth no worse a place.
> But he, as loving his own pride and purposes,
> Evades them with a bombast circumstance,
> Horribly stuffed with epithets of war,
> And in conclusion,
> Nonsuits my mediators. (1.1.8–16)

It can be difficult to feel much sympathy for someone so full of anger and resentment. And yet the precision with which Iago articulates his grievances here should make us consider how we would feel in his place. Iago is Othello's trusted officer. Unlike Cassio who "never set a squadron in the field," he is a seasoned warrior who has been present with Othello at past campaigns. But he is also unpolished and vulgar. He sees the lowest motives in everyone and suspects, on no apparent evidence, that both Othello and Cassio have slept with his wife.

What is apparent is that none of the other characters in the play "see" Iago, except in relation to their own grievances. He also happens to belong to the most invisible minority to educated readers of Shakespeare, who tend not to consider the fact that Iago has a valid grievance in being passed over and, perhaps most galling, in having that grievance go completely unnoticed. Othello's trust in Iago reflects, superficially, his admirably unsuspecting nature. But it also reflects how little he acknowledges Iago as a singular identity, a man with desires and ambitions who has been by his side for years. Even as Othello suffers from the bigotry of others, he demonstrates his own brand of blindness and prejudice toward Iago. Perhaps Iago is unworthy of promotion, but if he is, why would Othello be so susceptible to his counsel and so willing to trust him in his analysis of events?

It is worth saying a few words here about the transmutation, as I see it, of Shylock into Othello—of one marginal figure into another. Neither Jews nor Moors would probably have been known to Shakespeare beyond their stereotypical representation in his culture. Moors existed in some pockets of society (there is a record of Moorish ambassadors to England and of black musicians and entertainers, though no evidence of any in Shakespeare's circle). The threat of the "infidel" in the Mediterranean, where Othello goes to fight people of his own origin, was certainly present to English audiences. In addition, the slave trade had become an adjunct to discovery and conquest during this period, reinforcing prejudices against darker-skinned people.

Jews were even less likely to have crossed Shakespeare's path. There were effectively no Jews in England at the time he was writing. Although he may have encountered them if he visited Venice, we have no concrete evidence that he did. In his speculative study of Shakespeare's life, the critic Stephen Greenblatt suggests that he may have seen the hanging for treason of Queen Elizabeth's physician Roderigo Lopez, the son of a converted Jew, an event that could have spurred his sympathetic rendering of a Jewish character. But the connection seems to me far-fetched. I am more attached to the idea that the plot Shakespeare stumbled on for *The Merchant of Venice* encouraged him to imagine the inner workings of the Jewish character's mind, and that this, along with the instigation of Portia's remark about the Prince of Morocco's complexion, led him to move from the representation of a Jew to that of a black man—and from a humanized villain to a benighted hero. It is not that Jew and Moor are interchangeable in their marginality but rather that the imagination of one would lead a man of empathetic genius to imagine the other.

The shift from religion to color also had a practical value for the playwright. It allowed the exploration of the minority character to be grounded in appearance. Othello is a Christian (or, presumably, a Muslim who converted to Christianity); he functions like other Christians in the society, even if he does not look like them. Shylock, by contrast, may look like a Christian (were he to choose to do so), but his customs and beliefs separate him from them: "I will buy with you, sell with you, talk with you, walk with you, and so following; but I will not eat with you, drink with you, nor pray with you" (1.3.29–32). This dramatic expression of difference seems necessary in *The Merchant of Venice* to underline the difference that drives the plot but which in *Othello* can be represented visually by the dark skin (and, with few exceptions until recently, "blackface") of the character onstage.[2]

I should add that because Othello's Otherness is connected to the superficial fact of his skin color, this becomes a way of making the prejudice against him seem absurd. Despite the way productions in blackface have undercut this, the play seems to me to have great potential for combating racism. When we read closely, we are forced to feel for Othello and realize how much racial prejudice helped create his tragedy.

At the same time, while racial injustice springs into relief in the play, the injustice associated with class done to Iago has gone largely unnoticed. There is an irony in this. We tend to see color as a more burdensome deficit in our society. But it might be argued that its visual nature provides a clearer target, both to elicit bigotry and to combat it, than the more subtle and often invisible marginality that comes with lower-class status. This is an issue that colleges are struggling with in their admissions policies. It also explains why some members of the white working class are angry at what they see as race-related entitlements and are susceptible to Iago-like demagogues who take advantage of their sense of being passed over. If my students, white and black, give their hearts to Othello, my white students will sometimes admit that they see aspects of their parents or grandparents in Iago, and feel for him—understand his resentment better—by reading this play with close and unbiased attention.

8

King Lear

Age

*K*ing Lear is the only play in Shakespeare's canon that treats age as the Other—and the aged parent as both the protagonist and the antagonist. It is, in some respects, an extrapolation of *Hamlet*. If Hamlet is a man who struggles with the transition out of childhood, Lear is a man who struggles with the transition into old age, and this includes coming to terms with being the parent of adult children who are no longer under his control.

It seems to me impossible to think about the character of Lear without being reminded of an antecedent character, the only other aged character of note in Shakespeare's canon: Sir John Falstaff. Falstaff, of course, is a kind of Lear inversion. Though a knight, he has no ambition and no respect for authority. His speech against honor ("What is honour? A word. What is in that word honour? What is that honour? Air" [5.1.133–134]) lays out his philosophy. He devotes himself to prattle, pranks, drink, and an occasional robbery to remain solvent. But Falstaff does resemble Lear in that he occupies a paternal relationship to Prince Hal. While the death of Hal's biological father, Henry IV, makes possible Hal's ascendance to the throne, Falstaff, his pseudo-father, still remains to be dealt with. The severance occurs in *Henry IV, Part II*. After Hal has been crowned king, Falstaff calls out to him: "My king! my Jove! I speak to thee, my heart."—to which Hal responds, "I know thee not, old man" (5.5.44–45). This scene of repudiation invariably brings a tear to the eye of anyone who has felt sidelined or ignored by a loved one. Falstaff is a clownish figure who does not care for dignity or place in life, yet as an old man who is cruelly discarded, he must have made Shakespeare think about how a prouder, more self-important man would respond under similar circumstances. In Falstaff, we see an outline—albeit a very broad one—of the man who would become Lear.

Two additional hints of Shakespeare's empathetic feeling for old age can be found in *As You Like It*. The first concerns the character of Adam, servant to Orlando. When the two arrive in the Forest of Arden after being banished from their home, Adam, old and exhausted, announces that he "can go no further." Orlando hurries to assure him: "For my sake be comfortable; hold death awhile at the arm's end. I will here be with thee presently" (2.6.7–8). Orlando is kind. But what if he were less kind? What if he were *not* kind? Having reportedly played the part of Adam, Shakespeare might have been spurred to think more deeply about old age and the treatment of the elderly long after he had created the character.

The second hint is the "seven ages of man" speech that begins with the famous line: "All the world's a stage . . ." Delivered by the melancholic Jaques in act 2, the speech delineates each stage of human life in satirical terms, but moves, in the end, from satire to pathos:

Last scene of all
That ends this strange eventful history
Is second childishness, and mere oblivion,
Sans teeth, sans eyes, sans taste, sans everything.
(2.7.163–166)

These lines, in their wrenching portrayal of the end of life, can be said to project us forward to the elderly Lear, abused and turned out of doors, wandering mad and helpless in the storm.

As for the parental relationship so central to *Lear*, it has threaded its way through Shakespeare's canon from the beginning. Cruel, selfish, or at best clueless fathers, particularly of innocent daughters, are a motif in *Romeo and Juliet*, *Much Ado About Nothing*, *The Taming of the Shrew*, *Hamlet*, *Othello*, and *The Winter's Tale*. No doubt I am omitting other examples. But only in *The Merchant of Venice*, the play that provides the most hints for characters and themes that Shakespeare would develop later, does this kind of relationship occur on two fronts and, in one, involve the reciprocal selfishness and cruelty of the daughter. Portia's father has effectively maintained his control over her even after his death, dictating how her husband will be chosen, but it is the Shylock-Jessica relationship that I believe supplies the clue to *Lear*. A peripheral betrayal by a daughter of a tyrannical father in that earlier play is expanded in *Lear* to involve three daughters whose dramatic struggle with their father takes up the entire canvas.

As I have noted, the Shylock-Jessica plot in *The Merchant of Venice* was borrowed from another source in which the father and the daughter were not Jewish. Ascribing this plotline to his Jewish characters, Shakespeare was adding to the trauma Shylock suffered. Shylock's anguish humanized his character but compromised the plot in its comic aspect, an irregularity that may well have inspired Shakespeare's return to the issue in undiluted tragic form in *Lear.*

Let me reiterate my conviction that Shakespeare was supremely attuned to loose ends and dissonant tonalities. What was left unresolved or out of sync disturbed his imaginative tranquillity. *Lear* is his recasting of the tyrannical but also wronged father from a peripheral role in *The Merchant of Venice* to a central one. It discards ethnic Otherness—a condition that envenoms Shylock and conditions his daughter to despise him—and concentrates on the bare bones of age as a form of Otherness that alienates the individual from himself and from his children.

Lear is about many things, but ultimately it is a play about old age—how it feels to those who experience it and how it is responded to by those who are younger and tend not to realize that they too will one day be old. Old age is a stage at which most people hope to arrive in life but can hardly imagine until they reach it. Shakespeare was forty-two when he wrote *Lear,* not old by our standards, though life expectancy was much shorter then and he would die at fifty-two. But regardless of how relatively old or young we consider Shakespeare to have been when he wrote the play, it seems clear that his genius resided in the ability to imagine—and empathize with— what he did not directly experience. He could imagine the elderly Lear as he could imagine the Jewish Shylock and the black Othello.

Moreover, what must have spurred him to take up *Lear's* plot was that he was the father of adult children. What makes this play so productive for me to teach at this point in my life is that I too have adult children, and I can use my students, whose relationship to their parents parallels my children's to me, to reenact its central issues. As a class, we can examine the distance separating Lear from his daughters by thinking about the distance that separates my students from me. We can share our different perspectives, drawing on our positioning across the generational divide.

The first scene of *Lear* is key to embarking on such a discussion. When I teach the play, we spend at least one class—sometimes more—on this scene. Why would a powerful king decide to give up his kingdom to his daughters but before he did so order them to tell him how much they loved him? Lear's demand is both ridiculous—an artificial performance for the sake of his vanity—and also understandable: a deeply moving plea for attention with which any parent with grown children can identify.

My students inevitably split into two groups with respect to Lear's demand that his daughters tell him how much they love him. One group agrees with Cordelia; these students cannot understand Lear's need to have love expressed in a public, performative way. The other group sides with Goneril and Regan (at least as they appear at the outset); these students see no reason why a child should refuse to humor an aged father with the response he wants, whether what they say is entirely true or not. One could argue that the first group gives Lear more respect by resenting his demand, while the second, by placating him, dismisses him. But one could also say that the former group is crueler and the latter more kind. In both cases, there is a sense that a parent who behaves the way Lear does is either mentally unhinged or pathetically needy. At first encounter, Lear does not appear to be a cruel man, though he will act cruelly toward Cordelia later in this scene.

The traditional critical consensus has been to agree with Lear's pronouncement to Kent in act 3 that he is "more sinned against than sinning" (3.2.60). But I am not so sure. While it is true that two of his daughters, particularly the merciless Regan, are sociopaths, a close reading of the first scene suggests that they have learned their behavior from their father. Even Cordelia, as I shall argue, has a dose of cruelty in her disposition that she must have learned through example.

Lear has created the daughters he deserves, much as the cruel actions of Antonio created the Jewish moneylender he deserved in *The Merchant of Venice*. We can deduce this from Lear's opening demand to his daughters:

> Tell me, daughters
> (Since now we will divest us both of rule,
> Interest of territory, cares of state),
> Which of you shall we say doth love us most,
> That we our largest bounty may extend
> Where nature doth with merit challenge? (1.1.46–51)

When I referred earlier to Lear's request of his daughters, I generalized it in the way most people do when they recall this precipitating moment in the play. They say that Lear asks his daughters to tell him how much they love him. But this is not accurate. The question is not "How much does each of you love me?" but "Which of you loves me most?"

What must strike a close reader or listener of this line is not only the foolishness of Lear's demand—to expect verbal praise as recompense for a material gift and to imagine that he can dictate love in a quid pro quo fashion—but also the terms in which it is made: Lear has staged a *competition* among his daughters in anticipation of his gift giving. I should add that, though it might seem as if the competition would influence the size of the gift, this is not the case. The division of land has already been worked out in advance, and each daughter has been apportioned an equal share of his kingdom. Clearly, he wants their responses not to guide him in his gift giving but as a competitive performance. Even though he has already settled on an equitable division of his kingdom, he requires his daughters to compete for his favor.

These actions speak volumes about the kind of father Lear has been. He has raised his daughters to compete among themselves as the chosen method of pleasing him. Not only does he demand that his children make a competitive performance of their professions of love; he demands that this performance be enacted in front of a large audience. Combining competition with the potential for public humiliation is a recipe for filial and inter-sibling resentment.

The subsequent brutal acts that Goneril and Regan engage in seem to be the product of this conditioned behavior and of the resentment it has generated. Even their cruelty is competitive, each vying with the other to see how badly she can treat their father (for example, in the number of followers that they demand he eliminate from his retinue, with the vicious Regan going farthest in throwing him out of her house altogether). Their vitriol is ultimately turned against each other, as they compete to the death for the same man: Goneril poisons Regan and then commits suicide.

But what about Cordelia? She is presumably Lear's "favorite"—a fact reiterated by Kent, Goneril, Regan, and Lear himself at different junctures. To be the favorite of a father like Lear is a dubious honor. Families have odd ways of redressing imbalance, and those who seem to reap the greatest benefits can often pay in covert or indirect ways, as family therapists will attest. Cordelia is a dramatic example of someone who pays the penalty for her father's favoritism.

In the competition that Lear sets up, Cordelia ostensibly positions herself outside the fray. Her first words are an aside to the audience: "What shall Cordelia speak? / Love, and be silent" (1.1.60). When forced to respond, she answers in the opposite way from her sisters:

> You have begot me, bred me, loved me. I
> Return those duties back as are right fit,
> Obey you, love you, and most honour you.
> Why have my sisters husbands, if they say
> They love you all? Happily, when I shall wed,
> That lord whose hand must take my plight shall carry
> Half my love with him, half my care and duty.
> Sure, I shall never marry like my sisters. (1.1.94–101)

What must be noted here is that, while *seeming* to opt out of the competition that Lear sets up among the sisters, Cordelia ultimately *does* compete—and win—because she gets to her father in a way they cannot. Her coldly rational response—morbidly truthful, a parent might argue—rouses him to anger and irrational action. Yes, she is banished and disinherited, but she also proves, by inspiring such extreme action, that she can undermine her father's planned scenario and indirectly ensure his punishment. If Lear has used power and manipulation to raise his daughters, then this youngest and best loved has learned how to use these lessons against him, if unconsciously and reflexively. Indeed, it makes sense that the favorite daughter would be most profoundly influenced by his competitive style. Note, for example, that Cordelia has made a point of denigrating her sisters—not just their response to their father's demand but also their marriages ("I shall never marry like my sisters"). I would add that her idea that love can be apportioned (when she marries half her love will go to her husband) is a rationed concept of love, bred out of competitive conditioning. Indeed, one way of reading this play is as a competitive battle to the death between a father and his favorite daughter, whom he has trained to think the way he does.[1]

The bad parenting, exemplified in one form by Lear, takes a different form in a secondary character, the Earl of Gloucester, whose fate parallels Lear's. In the opening scene of the play, the Earl introduces his illegitimate son, Edmond, to Lear's loyal courtier, Kent: "His breeding, sir, hath been at my charge. I have so often blushed to acknowledge him, that now I am brazed to't" (1.1.8–10). Although the Earl of Gloucester goes on to say that he loves his illegitimate son as much as his legitimate one, his opening words always appall my students, who are shocked that a father would express shame about his son's birth in front of that son. They argue that this kind of speech is clearly second nature to the father, and the son has become inured to it. And yet, becoming accustomed to being treated as an embarrassment would not prevent—indeed, might encourage—the creation of deep-seated resentment, a feeling that the world owes the son, who engenders such shame, redress for the wound he has suffered in his illegitimacy. Thinking back to *Richard III,* we can see an evolution from the way Shakespeare represents Richard's deformity to the way he represents Edmond's illegitimacy. In Richard's case, we learn nothing more than that "dogs bark at me as I halt by them"; in Edmond's, we learn more about the human element that shaped him—from birth he has been a constant source of shame to his father.

Is this why Edmond is evil? Shakespeare has him later take full responsibility for his villainy: "I should have been that I am had the maidenliest star in the firmament twinkled on my bastardising" (1.2.120–123). Yet it is not the stars that have shaped Edmond; it is, rather, the conditions in which he exists, which include the conditions in which he has been shaped from childhood on. If Edmond is a self-generated villain in some respects, his last words express a well of profound neediness. "Yet Edmond was beloved" (5.3.213), he announces as he expires, referring to the deadly rivalry of Lear's daughters Goneril and Regan over him. The pathos of Edmond's final proclamation must recall his father's denigrating reference in the opening scene and remind

us how much a parent can wound a child not only through ego-
tistic manipulation like Lear's but through simple thoughtlessness
and self-indulgence. The Earl of Gloucester meant well enough
in bringing up his sons, but he was oblivious to the way his words
might deform a child's sense of self and how that same obliviousness would make him an easy prey to that child's manipulation
of him to destructive ends. One thinks here of the way Othello
created resentment in Iago not out of malice but out of blindness.
It is fitting in this context that the Earl of Gloucester, blind to his
sons in different ways, eventually suffers blindness by the order
of Lear's cruelest daughter, Regan.

Both Goneril and Regan, on the one hand, and Cordelia,
on the other, bring us back to the forces that pull human character in two directions. This dichotomy was dramatized in the
positioning of Hamlet between Claudius and Horatio. Claudius was a self-serving pragmatist whose behavior was strategic
and forward-seeking. Horatio was a moral rationalist whose
behavior was static and reductionist. Goneril and Regan are
like the former, Cordelia more like the latter. Lear is responsible
for these extremes, having created his daughters through his
egotistical, competitive parenting. Now, however, he can no
longer exert the power that once governed and directed their
extremism. He is at the mercy of his creations.

One of the truisms I extract from the play is that we get
the children we deserve. I cannot emphasize enough how much
this point comes to the fore in a discussion of *Lear* with students.
I see, as they discuss the play, the extent to which they are the
product of their upbringing. Lear is always familiar to them in
some way—even the most devoted children see some element
of their parents in him, much as they invariably see something
of their parents in Willy Loman—usually, though not always,
their father—when they read *Death of a Salesman*. Judging
from what they say and from my own experience, I see that

parenting is, inevitably, to some extent both coercive and oblivious, part Lear, part the Earl of Gloucester. We forgive our parents, if we can, and, if we are parents, learn to forgive ourselves.

But let me return to the central focus of this book: the way in which Shakespeare came to empathize with the outsider figure. Lear is one such figure. Whereas the psyches of Shylock and Othello have been twisted by the ongoing abuse they suffer in Venetian society, Lear only comes to inhabit his outsider role late in life. Taking this into account, we can realize that being empathetic to other kinds of marginality could prepare us for it when in old age we become marginal ourselves. It can also help us realize that if we are abusive to others in our youth, when we have vitality and power, we are likely to be retaliated against by those we abused when we are weak and expendable.

Lear resembles Richard II in being a powerful figure who must come to terms with losing power. But while Richard undergoes usurpation—a seemingly unnatural loss—Lear undergoes a natural process of diminishment that is made more painful because he cannot accept its inevitability. Used to being the center of attention and privilege, he goes through the motions of accepting a lesser role but without a true acceptance of what such a role really means.

What Lear endures seems to be the nightmare realization of what he might have feared would be in store: violent and extreme dismissal by those who once deferred to him. As he clutches at the vestiges of his former status while his daughters progressively reduce his retinue of knights to none, he literally puts himself out into the storm toward the end of act 2:

> I abjure all roofs, and choose
> To wage against the enmity o' the air,

To be a comrade with the wolf and owl,

Necessity's sharp pinch! (2.4.201–204)

There is an argument to be made that, even in extremis, Lear has not learned his lesson. His ordeal in the storm is his way of maintaining centerstage. He dramatically holds to that position in the context of the play as he suffers and rails against his daughters' cruelty. This is Shakespeare's understanding of how old age can feel to those conditioned to primacy in all previous aspects of their lives. Even when our power ebbs, we create drama based on our marginalization. (I realize that this argument conveniently sidesteps the fact that the play is *about* old age and thus requires that the old man be its center.)

But Lear's continued centrality fails to account for his emotional relationship to Cordelia. She has already, in a sense, punished him—forcing him to act like a despot toward her by not giving him what he asked for. At first he is unable to accept her refusal to play his game; later he gets back at her through his intense suffering and abuse at her sisters' hands. I am reminded of the demanding mother who wants attention from her child and gets it by becoming gravely ill. (This trope inevitably plays well, but it can also be overused and often satirized: "Mom, how are you?" "I'm dying, but other than that, I'm fine.")

What finally stops the cycle of manipulation is Cordelia's death, which ends the power struggle. There is no battle of wills possible when one player has left the field, and this is what happens at the end of *Lear*. He has no one to dominate, to insist upon centrality to, to demonstrate magnanimity or even penance toward. The moment of greatest pathos is his realization that Cordelia is dead and his performance in the game of life is over. He can only repeat the cry of a dying animal: "Howl, howl, howl, howl!" (5.3.231).

In his struggle for self-assertion in the face of opposition, Lear reminds me of Richard III. But Richard never fully accepts his loss of power. His battle is never about a relationship with anyone outside himself; no one touches him, and he dies without insight or repentance. Lear does achieve some kind of insight when he finally comprehends his love for Cordelia after he loses her.

I will conclude by saying that while I feel empathy for Lear, I do not actually pity him. My response may be connected to knowing my own tendency to be manipulative and histrionic as a parent. I am hard on myself and, by extension, hard on Lear.

I find that my students vary in their response to this character, depending, predictably, on their relationship with their own parents. Those who feel that their parents were neglectful or abusive of them tend to be hard on Lear. Those who feel their parents sacrificed everything for them tend to be most outraged on his behalf. But these are the extremes. Most students fall somewhere in between. They are both attached to and resentful of their parents, if only because they feel so dependent on them. They are therefore both appalled by Lear's treatment by his daughters and attuned to his manipulativeness and the way he might have helped shape their characters.

What I find so valuable about the play is its cautionary aspect. First, it teaches about the dangers of bringing competitive love into parenting—no one will profit from such a strategy in the long run. It also warns us of less dramatic forms of parental abuse reflected in the Earl of Gloucester's behavior toward Edmond. It is extremely hard for parents not to be thoughtless at times, not to indulge themselves and be oblivious to their children's feelings. But we know from psychologists that children pick up on cues that we may not realize we are giving them, and that patterns of response, begun early, can amplify and metastasize in crippling ways. This, I contend, is what occurs with Edmond. A basic sense of deprivation with regard to his father's love turns him into a monster who must satisfy that need through machination and seduction.

Finally, the play teaches us how important it is to step aside as we grow older, not just in form but in substance. Lear thought he was stepping aside when he gave away his kingdom, but his heart was not in it. We need to accept our marginality, to truly embrace being in the background rather than the foreground. This is a difficult lesson to learn for those of us who have had successful careers in the world or wielded authority in our households. Although *Lear* is about a father's ordeal, I would argue that mothers are perhaps more susceptible to some of the feelings associated with his situation. They are often the most involved in the raising of their children. During a long stretch of their lives, those children are dependent on them—until they aren't. Accepting a noncentral position can be both embarrassing to our public self ("I'm afraid Jeffrey can't make it to Thanksgiving this year") and painful to our private self ("Why doesn't he remember my birthday? Why doesn't he call more often?").

And yet because marginality and diminishment must come to us all, Shakespeare's great tragedy should help us accept these states of being, and in the process be more empathetic when we—and others—fall short.

9
Measure for Measure
A World Without Empathy

C ritics have labeled a handful of plays in Shakespeare's canon "problem plays": ethically ambiguous works that leave audiences wondering what the proper response to them should be.[1] *Measure for Measure* falls into this category. The play seems to be constructed for the express purpose of making it hard for us to get our bearings. Much of the difficulty seems to spring from a lack of empathy on the part of the characters for one another—and on the part of *us*, readers or viewers of the play, for them.

Measure for Measure is generally dated between or around the time of the great tragedies *Othello* and *Lear*, two plays of strong empathetic imagination. Yet *Measure for Measure* works not to arouse but to short-circuit feeling—to block our ability to feel warmth or compassion for its characters. It tacks a happy ending onto a set of depraved, manipulative, or unnaturally rigid characters. The play is important as a kind of hiatus in an evolution toward greater empathy that I see emerging as Shakespeare continued to write. We could, in fact, view it as a thought experiment: What would society be like if empathy were absent?

Shakespeare, as was his habit, borrowed the plot of *Measure for Measure*. The play is based on two sixteenth-century works: a story by the Italian Giraldi Cinthio (the author from whom he borrowed *Othello*) and a play by the English dramatist George Whetstone. There are several minor changes made to these borrowed plots and two important ones that I will refer to later.

Measure for Measure begins with Duke Vincentio, who announces that he will be traveling abroad on important business and has chosen to relegate his authority to Angelo, a man whom he publicly extolls as an exemplar of virtue. In reality, the Duke has no intention of going anywhere. He plans to live among his people disguised as a friar with the object, as he confesses to another friar, of rectifying the laxness with which he has ruled his kingdom: "We have strict statutes and most biting laws / . . . Which for these fourteen years we have let slip" 1.3.20, 22). He explains that if he were suddenly to become more stringent in the enforcement of these laws, " 'twould be my tyranny" (1.3.37)—that is, his people would resent him for changing course. But another leader, especially one with the virtuous character of Angelo, will be able to be strict.

Yet even as the Duke explains his rationale for the appointment of Angelo in his place, he adds a quibble that alerts us to the oddity of his plan. He ends with a second explanation for going undercover:

> Lord Angelo is precise,
> Stands at a guard with envy, scarce confesses
> That his blood flows, or that his appetite
> Is more to bread than stone. Hence shall we see,
> If power change purpose, what our seemers be. (1.3.51–55)

In other words, Angelo is put in charge both because of his apparent virtue and because the Duke has doubts about that virtue and wants to test it.

No sooner does Angelo assume his position than he begins enforcing a strict moral law. He arrests a young man named Claudio for getting his girlfriend, Juliet, pregnant, and condemns him to death, despite the fact that Claudio has every intention of marrying Juliet. Another character, Lucio, a debauched but loyal friend to Claudio, visits Claudio's sister, Isabella, asking her to intercede. Isabella is about to become a nun but agrees to leave her convent and plead for her brother's life. When she meets with Angelo, however, he is suddenly and unaccountably overcome with lust for her. He tells her that he will spare Claudio only if she will sleep with him.

Even in our cynical age, students react with shock to this plot turn.

Up until this point, the play has held more or less to its source materials, but Shakespeare now deviates from them. In the Cinthio and Whetstone plots, the sister of the condemned man, though disgusted and at first unwilling, finally submits to the proposition when her brother begs her to save his life. In *Measure for Measure*, however, the sister remains adamant in her refusal. "Better it were a brother died at once, / Than that a sister by redeeming him / Should die for ever" (2.4.107–109), she tells Angelo. And "More than our brother is our chastity" (2.4.186), she intones in her soliloquy directly following the encounter (a line that has gained a certain notoriety in its dramatic self-righteousness). She subsequently explains the offer to Claudio, expecting him to support her position, and when he pleads for his life instead she reacts with outrage:

> Oh, you beast!
> Oh faithless coward, oh dishonest wretch!

> Wilt thou be made a man out of my vice?
> Is't not a kind of incest to take life
> From thine own sister's shame?

The harangue continues, mounting to a hysterical crescendo:

> Take my defiance,
> Die, perish. Might but my bending down
> Reprieve thee from thy fate, it should proceed.
> I'll pray a thousand prayers for thy death,
> No word to save thee. (3.1.136–140, 143–147)

"'Tis best that thou diest quickly"(3.1.151), she concludes, an ironic statement given that Angelo has told her that if she does not acquiesce, he will prolong Claudio's death by torture.

No sooner does the encounter between Isabella and Claudio end, than the Duke, in his disguise as a friar, takes each of them aside, explaining that he has overheard what Angelo proposed. First he tells Claudio that Isabella was merely being tested by Angelo—that no reprieve is possible, and he must reconcile himself to death. Then he meets with Isabella and offers a solution to her dilemma. He suggests that they trick Angelo by having Mariana (a woman to whom Angelo was once engaged) take Isabella's place in his bed. This, he explains, would be a service to Mariana since it would force Angelo to marry her. The insertion of the "bed trick"—the substitution of one woman for another in the dark—is the second aspect of the plot that deviates from Shakespeare's sources.[2]

Both Isabella and Mariana agree to the plan, and it is carried out. But Angelo, though he thinks he has slept with Isabella, reneges on his promise and plans to proceed with Claudio's execution. The Duke intercedes again, arranging for the substitution of the head of a "notorious pirate" who died in prison for that of Claudio. He does not reveal the trick, however, until the last scene of the play, allowing Isabella to think that her brother is dead so as "To make her heavenly comforts of despair, / When it is least expected" (4.3.104–105).

I have relayed the plot of the play in some detail because its twists and turns are central to the weirdness and discomfort it engenders. One could argue that Shakespeare was simply lazy when he wrote it—that it is a shallow bricolage made up of elements from other plays. There are soliloquies and motifs that echo *Hamlet, Othello,* and *Henry V; All's Well That Ends Well* also has a bed trick. But in all these cases, the use of these elements is different. *Measure for Measure* flattens and trivializes what in previous plays inspires empathy for at least some of the characters.

But I think this is the point. The play is not a sloppy exercise but a serious exploration of a world in which behavior is so extreme and irrational that it cannot elicit empathy. It raises the question, What kind of characters in what kind of society would behave as these characters do and have this alienating effect?

Angelo is, obviously, the most depraved member of the group, made all the more despicable by appearing to be the most virtuous. His soliloquy in act 2, when he tries unsuccessfully to pray after acknowledging his lust for Isabella, is reminiscent of the scene in *Hamlet* in which Claudius tries to pray but admits that he cannot. But Claudius, at least, is dealing with a situation after the fact, when he can do nothing to rectify his crime. Angelo is attempting to pray *before* he makes his offer to Isabella. Even if we were to excuse the lust that overtakes him, his subsequent reneging on his promise to pardon Claudio shows that his exaggerated appearance of virtue has curdled into depravity. (The last line of Shakespeare's Sonnet 94 becomes a gloss on the trajectory of Angelo's character: "Lilies that fester smell far worse than weeds.") He appears unable to empathize with any of the others, whom he sees only as a means to support his own needs and desires.

If Angelo's deviation from appearances is deeply disturbing, Isabella's moral rigidity is almost equally so. While we can understand a piety that values chastity highly, it is hard to understand someone who sees no room for hesitation in considering its value with respect to the life of a loved one. We might argue that this is a contemporary bias—that we are more apt to uncouple sexuality from morality than Shakespeare's contemporaries. But Claudio argues eloquently for the same point inside the play:

> What sin you do to save a brother's life,
> Nature dispenses with the deed so far
> That it becomes a virtue. (3.1.134–136)

The fact that Shakespeare's original sources show the sister agreeing to the proposal in order to save her brother also suggests that there was as little argument then as now that a human life was worth more than chastity. Isabella's lack of empathy for her brother is staggering.

Still, she is positioned as the heroine in the play, which makes any judgment against her difficult. Her problematic nature is compounded by the fact that she sees her brother as having committed a crime in sleeping with Juliet before marriage yet is quick to agree to the bed trick, which reduplicates that same act in order to solve her own dilemma.

As for the Duke, he has traditionally been understood as a providential figure who wanders among his people and sets things right. But close consideration of his behavior makes this hard to rationalize. For one thing, he already had evidence that Angelo was morally flawed when he placed him in charge. We discover this later when he tells Isabella that Angelo had jilted

Mariana when her dowry was lost at sea, maneuvering himself out of the relationship by circulating rumors about her virtue. The Duke also allows Isabella to believe that her brother has been killed by Angelo until the end of the play, when he presents the living Claudio as part of his "reveal." This delay may produce an impressive dramatic effect, but it is predicated on a lack of empathy for the sufferings of Isabella and Mariana in the interim.

Finally, the Duke's goal of creating a stricter regime is not only stalled in the face of Angelo's depravity but dramatically undermined by the pardons he distributes in the final scene, which include commuting the sentence of an unrepentant murderer who has been languishing in the prison for some time. This seems less like compassion than caprice or, perhaps more disturbing, a taste for dramatic spectacle at the expense of justice.

The final discordant note in this play involves the Duke's request/demand for Isabella's hand in marriage at the end. His proposal is to someone about to enter a convent who has shown a profound distaste for sex (except when performed by someone else to get her off the hook). Shakespeare, significantly, gives her no lines in reply.

The only way that I have been able to make sense of the play is to read it as an elaborate dramatization of social pathology. The major characters are all deviant in ways that reflect and shape the society they inhabit.

Angelo is put into a position of power because he is a factotum of virtue. The habit of righteousness has rendered him cold and aloof, only reachable by someone who presents herself as equally righteous. This would account for his repudiation of his fiancée. The Duke notes that Angelo rejected Mariana when her dowry was lost: he "swallowed his vows whole, pretending in her discoveries of dishonor" (3.1.218–219). Our tendency is to see his impugning of her honor as an excuse for being mercenary, but it seems more likely to be the other way around.

The dowry's loss supplies the excuse for rejecting someone whom he sees not as morally tainted but rather as morally undistinguished. Isabella, by contrast, supplies the moral superiority that incites his lust.

Mariana, for her part, is represented as a kind of inverse of Angelo: what "should have quenched her love, hath like an impediment in the current made it more violent and unruly" (3.1.231–232). Her eagerness to agree to the bed trick is not just a pragmatic move to gain social respectability through marriage but an opportunity to indulge a "violent and unruly" desire incited by ill treatment. It is a masochistic passion.

Isabella's virtuous rigidity is also pathological. Early in the play, she is given the rules of the convent she is about to enter and responds: "I speak not as desiring more [privileges], / But rather wishing a more strict restraint" (1.4.3–4). Her outrage at having to consider giving herself to Angelo in exchange for her brother's life complements Angelo's passionate desire for her as a morally superior being. In other words, her sense of self is connected to her exaggerated sense of virtue; his sexuality is activated by that virtue. In both cases, virtue is a fetish— whether to define identity or provide sexual gratification.

As for the Duke, one could say that his deviance is connected to a compulsion for surveillance and control. His determination to watch and manipulate from behind the scenes is prolonged and elaborated over the course of the play. His delay in revealing himself underlines his lack of empathy for the other characters, particularly the wronged women. Until the final scene, Isabella is allowed to think that her brother has been killed, and Mariana that her valid claim to marriage with Angelo has been dismissed. This is emotional cruelty of a high order. Even in the final scene, the Duke maintains his cover until his friar's hood is literally pulled off by Lucio, the play's most openly debauched and cynical character.

These characters all suffer from a serious deprivation of feeling for their fellow human beings. Such a disability might, under certain circumstances, render a person empathetic. (I happen to believe that this is the case for Shylock and even, sporadically, for Iago.) But given the centrality of Angelo and the Duke in the society they inhabit, any empathy we might feel for them is canceled. They are the product of their culture's ideology and the means by which this ideology is perpetuated. Even Isabella, insofar as she represents the holy life of the convent, has a generic authority.

A society predicated on "virtue-seeming" is bound to foster hypocrisy on the one hand and an unrealistic view of virtue on the other. A leader who spies on his citizens and manipulates justice to suit his purposes is bound to create a disrespect for the law. Mariana may fleetingly arouse our empathy, given her weakness and dependence in a society that has ostracized her. But if we consider Mariana in the context of both Angelo and the Duke's behavior, we could argue that both an extreme compliance and an unhealthy relationship to sexuality might also emerge from a society where empathy is in such short supply.

A predilection for subterfuge, hypocrisy, and sadomasochistic behavior is one of the key ingredients of an authoritarian state. For all that the Duke is lax in his enforcement of the law, the values that the play exhibits support the capricious exercise of power. His decisions at the end represent not justice or even mercy; they are a sweeping away of accountability for all concerned, a feel-good spectacle that plays well with an unreflective audience. The ending is the bread and circus of a dictator, though one masquerading in sheep's (or friar's) clothing.

In the context of the social deviance associated with the false virtue of the ruling class, the ordinary people in the play are its mirror: genuine ne'er-do-wells including pimps, prostitutes, and those who consort with them. The question becomes, Does the deviance of leadership give rise to the debauchery of the people? The Duke suggests that it does when he puts power in the hands of Angelo, hoping to see his subjects' disrespect for the law corrected by a more severe authority. The result, however, is, if anything, a reinforcement of what existed before and a means of better dramatizing the moral pathology of the ruling class, which exceeds that of its citizens. In this context, the lax populace becomes less a mirror of than a corrective to the deeper moral turpitude of the elite. These sinners at least are honest and above-board. Better to skirt the law with sexual license and other sorts of winking than espouse a high-minded virtue as a cover for underhanded vice and depravity.

I must end by noting that my students' response to this play when I taught it in the fall of 2019 took me by surprise. It diverged radically from the response of students in previous years. In the past, there was a consensus that Isabella was a religious zealot, attached to an idea of chastity that blinded her to a morally appropriate and empathetic course of action. Some found her selfish and cruel, others naive and addled by her religious training. In either case, my students strongly disapproved of her response. But in my most recent class—which happened to be made up mostly of women—a new kind of support appeared for her position. The first student to speak on the subject began her remarks as follows: "I find Isabella's determination to sacrifice her brother for her principle to be . . ."—I expected her to end her sentence with "reprehensible" or "wrong," but she instead concluded, "courageous and admirable." The rest of the class nodded in agreement. No one would condemn her. Even those who admitted they would act otherwise in her place refused to judge her. As one student explained, "I have a brother who I really love and, personally, I would agree to Angelo's bargain, but I respect Isabella for holding to what she believes and to her right to be in control of her own body."

The support for Isabella's position in 2019 is connected to a general tendency to see all three female characters—Isabella, Mariana, and Juliet—as victims of the patriarchy and to make their victimhood the primary focus of the play. Certainly, Shakespeare was attuned to the double standard facing women in his society. I have discussed this awareness as it informs *The Merchant of Venice* and *As You Like It*. In *Measure for Measure*, it is clearly present as well. At one point, the Duke asks Juliet if she was a willing participant in the relationship that resulted in her pregnancy; when she says she was, he asserts, "Then was your sin of heavier kind than his" (2.3.28). He also brutally questions Mariana at the end, pretending that he does not believe her claim against Angelo: "Why, you are nothing then: neither maid, widow, nor wife?" (5.1.177). Many critics have written about the demeaning nature of the bed trick, with its assumption that women are indistinguishable in the dark, a conceit that hearkens back to primitive notions of women as tokens of exchange between men.

But these ideas, which are critiques of patriarchal power and which I addressed in passing when teaching the play in previous years, have now gained new urgency in the context of the #MeToo and Time's Up movements. The quid pro quo that Angelo offers Isabella and his assertion that if she tells anyone about his proposition she will not be believed, echoes, at least superficially, the kinds of bargains that young women have had to deal with in all walks of life, and which are now being exposed and the perpetrators punished. My students maintained that for Isabella the stakes were even higher than they were for the young women in recent high-profile cases, and this made her especially courageous. Thus, where I see Isabella's placing of her own autonomy above Claudio's life as a failure of moral proportion and a deficit of empathy for her brother, they see moral heroism and are prompted to be more empathetic toward her.

I recently saw a production of the play that underlined the #MeToo aspect by making some minor changes in the last scene so that the Duke's demand for Isabella's hand in marriage occurs at the very end. In the play as Shakespeare wrote it, Isabella never answers the Duke's proposal, but in this production, she faces the audience before the curtain falls, and blurts out incredulously, "*What the fuck?!!!*"[3]

This revised staging fits with our recent awakening to the pervasiveness of sexual harassment and assault in our society. It also conforms to my recent students' support for Isabella's decision to control her body at all costs. And it tells us something about how a given historical moment can shape our response to people and situations. When one corner of life has been illuminated, we are likely to focus our attention and concern in that area and ignore or give short shrift to other areas that may have affected us deeply in the past. This explains the radical shift in my students' response to the play in the face of well-publicized, progressive ideologies.

I wonder whether my current students' feeling for Isabella is genuine or simply reflects knee-jerk support for the political principles popular with their peer group at the moment. Then again, is it fair for me to draw this kind of distinction—as though I know what genuine emotional responsiveness is and can separate it from political responsiveness? Perhaps I am dealing with my own failure of empathy, given the limitations of my own upbringing and education.

Whatever the reason, *Measure for Measure* is, for me, a play that does not inspire empathy for its characters, with the possible exception of Claudio, made desperate in the face of his sister's intransigence. But Claudio is a minor character and seems more of a plot device than a person we are meant to think and feel deeply about.

What the play does do, in my opinion, is unmask the deleterious effects of extremism in any form as something that tends to misshape both the individual and the society in which it is allowed to flourish; it short-circuits empathy and places us, rather like the Duke, in the position of detached onlooker. I worry that my current students' response reenacts the support for abstract principle over real human experience, and that it reflects the kind of unhealthy extremism the play is critiquing.

In the end we are left with the question, What constitutes virtue, and when does too much virtue become vice? This question is worth pondering in our current society, in which powerful men are being brought down by women whom they exploited under the cover of privilege, and in which women and men have turned the appearance of virtue into a competitive sport. Shakespeare's play encourages us to see ourselves in the rigidity, self-righteousness, hypocrisy, sadomasochism, and voyeuristic manipulativeness of its characters.

There is a morbid mirroring of our worst impulses represented in this play that makes me see it as an attempt to explore what the world would be like if empathy were absent. It reflects, perhaps, a disaffected interlude in Shakespeare's career, or at least a decision not to exert the kind of effort that enriched the characters in previous plays. It comes as a relief, therefore, to put it behind us and to see its dramatic antithesis in the great empathetic human drama *Antony and Cleopatra*.

10

Antony and Cleopatra
Wider Vistas

I am tempted to call *Antony and Cleopatra* a late-life rewrite of *Romeo and Juliet*. The feuding Montagues and Capulets are replaced by the feuding Egypt and Rome; the young star-crossed adolescent lovers by equally fated mature and powerful leaders. If we took the dialogue early in act 1 out of context we might think that this play was recycling the high-flown romantic language of *Romeo and Juliet*. Compare Juliet's: "My bounty is as boundless as the sea, / My love as deep; the more I give to thee / The more I have, for both are infinite" (2.2.133–135) with the following:

> CLEOPATRA: If it be love indeed, tell me how much.
> ANTONY: There's beggary in the love that can be reckoned.
> CLEOPATRA: I'll set a bourn how far to be beloved.
> ANTONY: Then must thou needs find out new heaven, new earth. (1.1.14–17)

Yet this dialogue is only a small piece of a larger drama in which high-flown sentiments are continually being undermined or betrayed. No sooner do Antony and Cleopatra dramatically declare their love than Antony returns to Rome, where he quickly agrees to marry Octavia, sister to his partner in the triumvirate Octavius Caesar. Later in the play, Cleopatra also comes close to betraying Antony to save herself. The love these characters feel for each other seems authentic but also deeply flawed and liable to contradiction. The empathy we feel for them is therefore more complicated than what we feel for Romeo and Juliet or even for more uninflectedly flawed characters like Othello and Lear. We see these later lovers as not so much tragically flawed as supremely human, heroic emblems of a condition of being which invariably includes weakness and failure.

The play begins by immediately presenting a contrast between the pleasure-loving, artful Egypt of Cleopatra and the disciplined, results-oriented Rome under the ruling triumvirate of Octavius Caesar, Lepidus, and Antony. Antony, however, unlike the cold-blooded, strategic Caesar or the foolish, oblivious Lepidus, has begun to stray from the expectations of his role. We learn about this in the first lines of the play, spoken by a Roman soldier, reporting on Antony's infatuation with Cleopatra:

> Nay, but this dotage of our general's
> O'erflows the measure. Those his goodly eyes,
> That o'er the files and musters of the war
> Have glowed like plated Mars, now bend, now turn
> The office and devotion of their view
> Upon a tawny front. His captain's heart,
> Which in the scuffles of great fights hath burst
> The buckles on his breast, reneges all temper
> And is become the bellows and the fan
> To cool a gipsy's lust. (1.1.1–10)

Antony has not simply become debauched, as depicted here; he has allowed himself to be misled, fallen under the sway of the Other: "a tawny front," a "gipsy." Cleopatra is far more profoundly Other than Juliet. The stubborn, one-note passion that makes *Romeo and Juliet* such a romantic but also such a juvenile play is replaced by something more erratic in *Antony and Cleopatra*. The terms in which the main characters engage are more complicated and profound.

The lure of Cleopatra is described in act 2 by Antony's right-hand man, Enobarbus. When it is suggested that his master, having married Caesar's sister Octavia, must now leave Cleopatra "utterly," he replies:

> Never. He will not.
> Age cannot wither her, nor custom stale
> Her infinite variety. Other women cloy
> The appetites they feed, but she makes hungry
> Where most she satisfies. For vilest things
> Become themselves in her, that the holy priests
> Bless her when she is riggish. (2.2.246–252)

The passage is a wonderful paeon to difference—to the ability to continually change and mutate and, as result, to turn established customs and beliefs on their head.

But while Cleopatra's changeableness is inherent to her nature—driven, as my students often argue, by her need to survive as a powerful woman in a male world—Antony's shifts are ostensibly the result of divided loyalties between Egypt and Rome. We have seen divided loyalties before, most notably in *Henry IV*, where Prince Hal vacillates between the duty-bound world of his father and the pleasure-seeking world of Falstaff. But Antony is not a boy; he is a man, seasoned in life and love. His oscillation between Egypt and Rome therefore carries a different meaning.

Given my conviction that Shakespeare was continually led to expand on characters whose outline he had sketched but not filled in in previous works, I believe that he was inspired to create Antony after having created Angelo in *Measure for Measure.* An abstraction of a virtuous man at the beginning, Angelo becomes an uninflectedly corrupt one at the end. This is a simplistic fall from smug self-righteousness to lustful self-indulgence. But what happens when the idealized figure is a genuine hero who seems to betray the values associated with his heroism because he changes his allegiance toward what he thinks is important?

Caesar calls Antony an "old ruffian," a richly denigrating reference that both reflects the speaker's sense of superiority and highlights the subject's long and battle-scarred existence in the world. Antony's fall is not the result of a capricious attack of lust, as with Angelo. Instead, it emerges organically out of a life that was lived fully in one arena until a new one opened up to him. Antony articulates this early in act 1 in an ecstatic moment with Cleopatra:

> Let Rome in Tiber melt and the wide arch
> Of the ranged empire fall! Here is my space.
> Kingdoms are clay; our dungy earth alike
> Feeds beast as man. The nobleness of life
> Is to do thus (1.1.35–39)

Having glimpsed this transcendent vision, Antony can hardly return to his old life with much enthusiasm. Thus, his subsequent return to Rome seems less an equivocation than a falling back into routine behavior. His marriage to Octavia and the resumption of his role in the triumvirate seems to be a function of habit. He has had a Roman wife once before, and he has already fought many times on behalf of Rome, his courage and leadership proven again and again.

Rome is the trodden path, the known experience. Egypt is a new world: exciting, untried, unconventional. Under the sway of Cleopatra, Antony "bends" and "turns" from everything he had known before. The reference to her "tawny front" may put us in mind of Othello. But while Othello is the Other who exists inside Venetian society, Cleopatra is the Other who exists outside Roman society—and who lures Antony away from the values and experiences of Rome.

It helps that embedded in Antony's history is an openness to unconventional experience that provides the groundwork for what he chooses to do in the course of the play. One of the most telling passages is spoken by Caesar when he describes Antony's past exploits:

> Thou didst drink
> The stale of horses and the gilded puddle
> Which beasts would cough at. Thy palate then did deign
> The roughest berry on the rudest hedge.
> . . .
> On the Alps
> It is reported thou didst eat strange flesh,
> Which some did die to look on. (1.4.62–65, 67–69)

This extraordinary passage identifies Antony as a man capable of living outside the bounds of the known—of existing and even thriving in an entirely alien environment. It anticipates his attraction to Cleopatra, whose Otherness would frighten and intimidate ordinary men (though both Julius Caesar and Pompey, each in his way unconventional, had previously fallen under her spell).

As the comparison between Antony and Octavius Caesar is developed in the play, we are made to reassess the way we think about success and failure. The Egyptian soothsayer warns Antony to distance himself from Caesar:

> If thou dost play with him at any game,
> Thou art sure to lose; and of that natural luck
> He beats thee 'gainst the odds. Thy lustre thickens
> When he shines by. I say again, thy spirit
> Is all afraid to govern thee near him;
> But, he away, 'tis noble. (2.3.26–31)

Shakespeare borrows this warning from his source, Plutarch's *Life of Marcus Antonius,* but changes the weight he gives to the words. Plutarch makes reference to Antony's "fortune," which, he says, is "blemished and obscured by Caesar's fortune." Shakespeare refers to Caesar's "luck," a lighter and more colloquial term for fortune. But despite the soothsayer's remark, luck is not really at issue for Antony. Egypt is not a better site from which to overcome his antagonist; his luck will not necessarily change there. But it is a better site for the expression of a full identity: for the return of his "lustre" and his "spirit"—existential qualities more admirable than luck, and qualities that Octavius Caesar is entirely without. Caesar's success is the result of discipline and patience—the ability, one could say, to wait for Antony to make a mistake. Even his much-vaunted love for his sister Octavia reflects this: he sacrifices her to a marriage of convenience in the apparent hope of keeping the triumvirate together while also providing a pretext for waging war on Antony if he returns to Cleopatra.

A pivotal moment in the play occurs in act 3, when Antony, having definitively left Rome and Octavia, committing himself to Cleopatra, declares his determination to oppose Caesar in a battle at sea—when war on land is the obvious "winning" strategy. Antony's men implore him *not* to fight at sea, but he refuses to listen. Caesar, he says, "dares us to it" (though there is no indication that Caesar has done so), and Cleopatra wants him to do it. These are emotional rationales, not strategic ones.

Once the sea battle is under way, Cleopatra's ships turn and flee, and Antony's follow hers:

> She once being loofed,
> The noble ruin of her magic, Antony,
> Claps on his sea wing, and, like a doting mallard,
> Leaving the fight in height, flies after her.
> I never saw an action of such shame.
> Experience, manhood, honour, ne'er before
> Did violate so itself. (3.10.17–23)

This flight, described by a Roman soldier, gives us the events in Roman terms: it is a shameful violation of "experience, manhood, honour." But it can also be understood as an act of devotion. Antony gives himself to Cleopatra in the battle as he has given himself to her as a lover. He refuses to hold to the boundaries between public and private that would ordinarily dictate how men and women conventionally relate to each other. Antony's loss and shame make him empathetic to us in a new way. His flight expresses a willingness to be led by the loved one "to the very heart of loss" (4.12.29).

Antony's defeat can also be understood in the context of his having twice challenged Caesar to single combat. This kind of challenge is familiar to us from *Henry IV* and *Henry V*. In both cases, the challenge is presented by Prince Hal, later Henry V, as a way to save lives, but it seems like an empty gesture, and is predictably rejected. In *Antony and Cleopatra* the offer is even more empty, since Antony is in such an obviously weak position. But the capitulation at sea can be read in the context of that earlier challenge: Antony's decision to leave the battle and lose face keeps him from sacrificing more men.

This reading may seem a stretch; it so dramatically opposes the terms of warfare codified by Rome, where winning is the unquestioned ultimate goal. After his defeat, Antony's Roman identity reasserts itself, as he laments: "I have fled myself, and have instructed cowards / To run and show their shoulders" (3.11.8–9). This kind of thinking and rhetoric is again, I believe, reflexive, a function of his conditioning in the Roman values from which he is being increasingly lured away by Cleopatra.

Reading this play with close attention, we, like Antony, are being lured away from conventional notions of heroism. It presents us with a continual shifting of fortune during the battle, with as little as a line or two used to suggest an encounter in the battle happening in one scene that is canceled by another in the next. Acts 3 and 4 have thirteen and fifteen scenes, respectively. The back-and-forth acts as a wide zoom on the events, disrupting a coherent trajectory toward victory or defeat. Antony fights again after his loss at sea and wins, then fights again and loses. His men desert him. We learn that one pillar of the Roman triumvirate, Lepidus, has been betrayed by Caesar and that Pompey has been murdered at Antony's order (an act regretted later, since he might have been Antony's ally against Caesar). Both these events happen offstage and are relayed as afterthoughts. Pompey's death is especially ironic since in act 2 he hosted a party on board his ship to celebrate a truce with Antony, Lepidus, and Caesar, during which one of his men took him aside and asked, "Wilt thou be lord of all the world?" (2.7.60)—a suggestion that he ignore the truce and cut the throats of the triumvirate leaders. Pompey refused the offer out of a sense of honor, but, we now learn, he has since suffered the results of his high-mindedness. How much less costly in arms and men, how much more beneficial to himself would an acceptance of his subordinate's offer have been? We are being shown along with Antony that ideas of honor and precedence— even victory—are arbitrary and hollow values.

Perhaps the most vivid moment of revisionism in the play comes when Antony bungles his own suicide, a coda to his loss at sea. Dying by one's own hand is the Roman way of dealing with defeat, but Antony does not carry it off with the sort of efficiency we would expect of a great general. First he asks his servant, the freed slave Eros, to kill him, and Eros, unwilling to do so, kills himself. Antony then stabs himself without completing the job and must be carried to the monument in which Cleopatra has confined herself and be hoisted up to bid her a last-gasp farewell. It seems almost comic that he cannot get this final act of leave-taking right. There is a degree of slapstick in the play that interpenetrates with the most dire calamities—a cosmic sense of humor, one could say, that forces us to see beyond the conventional conflict between the warring characters to the larger picture in which such things dwindle in significance. The bungled suicide is both farcical and profound. It makes clear that though dying can be dressed up as noble and valuable to posterity, it is in reality messy and without enduring value. The idea was already present in Falstaff's famous "honor" speech in *Henry IV, Part I* ("What is that 'honour'? Air."), and it is more fully dramatized in the same play when Hotspur is defeated in battle by Hal. His dying words reiterate that character's "Roman" values:

> O Harry, thou hast robbed me of my youth!
> I better brook the loss of brittle life
> Than those proud titles thou hast won of me.

But these words are followed by lines that qualify if not negate them:

> O, I could prophesy,
> But that the earthy and cold hand of death

Lies on my tongue. No, Percy, thou art dust,
And food for— *(He dies.)* (5.4.76–78, 82–85)

The sentence is finished by Hal: "For worms, brave Percy. Fare
thee well, great heart! / Ill-weaved ambition, how much art thou
shrunk" (5.4.86–87). While the killing of Hotspur allows Hal
to prove himself to his father and prepares him to take over as
king, the fact that the great warrior is now "food for worms"
points us forward to *Antony and Cleopatra*. One could argue
that Antony remains, despite himself, tied rhetorically to the
values that his actions repudiate as Cleopatra, after his death,
builds him into a mythic figure:

Nature wants stuff
To vie strange forms with fancy; yet t'imagine
An Antony were Nature's piece 'gainst fancy,
Condemning shadows quite. (5.2.96–99)

This elaborate twist on the relationship between fact and fancy,
reality and imagination places Antony in a new sphere—as a
new creation of Shakespeare's imagination. Given what we have
seen of his fall, we now understand that he is a man who is able
to abase himself, to act the fool, to refuse to resent or retaliate,
and to be afraid of death and unable to effect it simply. Antony's
final greatness is built on an imperfect love that can withstand
weakness and failure. Sonnet 138 is the poem most often associated with this play, worth citing in its entirety for its understanding of a love that relies on even as it sees through the
flattering lies that make life bearable:

When my love swears that she is made of truth,
I do believe her though I know she lies,
That she might think me some untutored youth,

Unlearnèd in the world's false subtleties.
Thus vainly thinking that she thinks me young,
Although she knows my days are past the best,
Simply I credit her false-speaking tongue;
On both sides thus is simple truth suppressed.
But wherefore says she not she is unjust?
And wherefore say not I that I am old?
O, love's best habit is in seeming trust,
And age in love loves not to have years told.
Therefore I lie with her and she with me,
And in our faults by lies we flattered be.

The sonnet expresses the wisdom of mature experience. To get
older is to decline. When death is within view, small gestures
can mean more than high-flown heroic behavior. "Give me
a kiss. / Even this repays me" (3.11.69–70), says Antony as he
confronts Cleopatra in the face of his cowardice and defeat.

Where does this leave the reader emotionally? As I noted
in my Introduction, classical tragedy is supposed to produce
catharsis—an outpouring of pity and fear for the heroic protagonist that cleanses us of repressed or unlocalized emotion. I
have defined empathy as a special kind of catharsis that causes
us to feel beyond ourselves for those outside the realm of our
experience. But in the case of Antony, the empathetic focus has
shifted. Antony is not an Other like Shylock, Othello, Lear, or
even Hamlet. He is a hero who loves an Other, who engages in
an extreme form of what we do in feeling for these earlier characters. In the way he loves Cleopatra, he models not just feeling
but action. In being at once an insider—a consummate Roman—
and an "ally" to an outsider,[1] he is able to recalibrate our sense
of what matters as we navigate our life's journey toward death.
By willfully placing himself outside the norms of his society and
attaching himself passionately to someone so different from

himself—a woman, a queen, a "tawny front," a "gipsy"—he redefines what it means to be a hero.

Romeo and Juliet, the product of the playwright's youth, gives us star-crossed lovers produced through the obliviousness and unintentional cruelty of their feuding families. We feel that these lovers were cheated of a life together. This is the tragedy of the play.

*Antony and Cleo*patra, however, deals with protagonists in both a wider and a later context. They are great leaders and, if not old, like Lear, well past their "salad days"—that is, old enough to have loved many times before, and close enough to death to understand its inevitability. In both *Romeo and Juliet* and *Antony and Cleopatra* the mistaken death of one character leads the other to kill himself, but the mistake functions very differently in the two plays. In *Romeo and Juliet,* the mistake seems a cruel twist of fate. The play would have been a festive comedy were it not for bad timing. In *Antony and Cleopatra,* bad timing has no real bearing on the outcome. The protagonists are fated to die, and Cleopatra's pretense that she is dead, precipitating Antony's decision to kill himself, merely brings things to their conclusion more quickly and efficiently. Their deaths, the inevitable coda to their love, mark the counterpoint to the cold, dull existence that has become associated with Octavius Caesar and Rome.

I am inclined to gloss the situation of *Antony and Cleopatra* by jumping ahead in time to Matthew Arnold's lyrical plaint in "Dover Beach":

> Ah, love, let us be true
> To one another! for the world, which seems
> To lie before us like a land of dreams,
> So various, so beautiful, so new,

> Hath really neither joy, nor love, nor light,
> Nor certitude, nor peace, nor help for pain;
> And we are here as on a darkling plain
> Swept with confused alarms of struggle and flight,
> Where ignorant armies clash by night.

While it is arguable that Antony and Cleopatra are consistently "true to one another," their love seems nonetheless intense and real, especially when placed against the "confused alarms of struggle and flight" of the armies that clash in the background. By the same token, their courage and dynamism, their movement across wider vistas, make them more heroic and inspiring than Arnold's punier, more desperate lovers.

It must be acknowledged in closing that while *Antony and Cleopatra* is by far the more profound exploration of love and death, *Romeo and Juliet* is the more effective piece of theater. The latter is performed regularly, not just by repertory companies but in high schools and even middle schools; the former is rarely performed at all. This tells us something about the evolution of Shakespeare's creative imagination—his tendency to push beyond what he had accomplished with regard to dramatic form as well as character delineation. *Antony and Cleopatra* is less a great play than a great proto-cinematic work; it seems to call out for flashbacks, montage effects, and camera zooms. It surprises me that a master filmmaker—a Steven Spielberg—has not yet attempted to render it on-screen or in a TV mini-series. The 1963 cinematic blockbuster *Cleopatra*, starring Elizabeth Taylor and Richard Burton in the throes of a tempestuous real-life love affair, for all that it makes no use of Shakespeare's text, comes closest to channeling the messy, vibrant, empathetic quality of that late Shakespearean tragedy.

It is the *un*theatrical nature of *Antony and Cleopatra* that, I would argue, leads directly into Shakespeare's last plays, which deviate markedly from previous generic constraints. These plays were written to be performed in a new, more intimate space, the Blackfriars theater. They incorporate masques—interludes of dance and music—and stylized effects involving magic and transformation; both form and content take a new turn. Of these plays, *The Winter's Tale* seems the most emblematic and intriguing. One could say that on arrival at this play near the end of his writing career and his life, Shakespeare had most completely and satisfyingly evolved.

11

The Winter's Tale

Across Generations

*T*he *Winter's Tale* is the penultimate play in Shakespeare's canon. It is followed by *The Tempest,* the play that seems to close his writing life. "I'll break my staff, / Bury it certain fathoms in the earth, / And deeper than did ever plummet sound / I'll drown my book" (5.1.54–57), announces Prospero in what has been understood to be its creator's declaration that he will stop writing and retire to his native Stratford-on-Avon. *The Tempest* presents a benignly fantastic, neatly structured world that is a comforting finale to an extraordinary creative career: lessons are learned, sins are forgiven, the fathers retire, and their children lead us forward into a "brave new world" (5.1.183).

The Winter's Tale is ostensibly like *The Tempest* in its fairy-tale quality. Like its successor, it is set in exotic, imaginary locales, contains magical or seemingly magical elements and coincidences, and mixes references to a classical pagan past with more contemporary Christian allusions. But *The Winter's Tale* is a more disturbing and challenging play than *The Tempest.* It addresses more directly and harrowingly, if also more forgivingly, the themes that dominated the great tragedies, *Hamlet, Othello,* and *Lear:* nostalgia for the past, rivalry between friends, incitements to jealousy and revenge, and the blindnesses and moral pitfalls attached to parenting. Like *Measure for Measure* and *Antony and Cleopatra,* though without the shallowness of the former or the grandiloquence of the latter, it also deals with sin and forgiveness.

Yet while *The Winter's Tale* looks back to earlier great plays, it also diverges from them in the breadth of its perspective. It is divided between events that occur in one locale, and those that occur in another sixteen years later, although the action returns at the end to where it began. Shakespeare has a figure personifying Time address the audience at the beginning of act 4 to announce the passage of a generation. The play builds the long view on human life into its structure.

The drama is instigated in act 1 by a fit of jealousy that seems to irrationally take hold of Leontes, King of Sicilia. He accuses his wife, Hermione, of infidelity with his best friend, Polixenes, King of Bohemia, who has been visiting Sicilia for nine months. Everyone is shocked by the accusation, and all protest vociferously that it is not true. But Leontes remains fixed in his conviction. Polixenes is forced to flee back to his native Bohemia in fear for his life; Hermione is sent to prison, where she gives birth to a daughter whom Leontes is convinced was fathered by his friend. He orders the baby be taken into the wilderness to die. When a message arrives from the Oracle of Delphi announcing Hermione's innocence, Leontes dismisses it as false. He then learns that his young son Mamillius has died of grief at seeing his mother abused, and, directly following, is told that Hermione, hearing the news of her son's death, has collapsed and been pronounced dead by Paulina (self-described as Leontes' servant, physician, and counselor). These deaths, following directly upon Leontes' defiance of the Oracle, finally bring him to his senses. He emerges from his paroxysm of jealousy and prepares to do penance for the rest of his life under the guidance of Paulina.

The first three and a half acts of the play are an extraordinary feat of compression. So much occurs so quickly, and yet, unlike the contrived events in *Measure for Measure* where no explanation or retribution is given for the egregious actions performed by the characters, this play is acutely concerned with what propels such actions, with punishment, and ultimately with forgiveness.

Leontes' jealousy, which seems to erupt out of nowhere, is in fact jealousy of *both* his wife *and* his best friend. His deep feeling for Polixenes can be extrapolated from Polixenes' own description of their boyhood together:

> We were as twinned lambs that did frisk i' th' sun
> And bleat the one at th' other. What we changed
> Was innocence for innocence; we knew not
> The doctrine of ill-doing, nor dreamed
> That any did. Had we pursued that life
> And our weak spirits ne'er been higher reared
> With stronger blood, we should have answered heaven
> Boldly, "not guilty," the imposition cleared
> Hereditary ours. (1.2.66–74)

The friendship as described here was a kind of Eden—a state of innocence and oneness—whose loss comes with being "higher reared / With stronger blood." Polixenes goes on to explain to Hermione that this change is due in part to the introduction of women into their lives:

> for
> In those unfledged days was my wife a girl;
> Your precious self had then not crossed the eyes
> Of my young playfellow. (1.2.77–80)

The scenario recalls Hamlet's dilemma: his nostalgia for an innocent childhood and his resentment against his mother and
Ophelia for their roles in awakening him to adult sexuality.

But the loss of innocence that Polixenes describes and that
underlies Leontes' eruption of jealous rage is not only or even
primarily related to sexuality. It is also connected to the emer-
gence of a new competitiveness between once noncompetitive
boys. Shakespeare dramatizes this element in the first scene. As
is common in many of his plays, he supplies an oblique key to
the drama at the outset. Here, representatives of Sicilia and
Bohemia are shown discussing the hospitality that their kings
feel obliged to show each other:

> Sicilia cannot show himself overkind to Bohemia.
> They were trained together in their childhood; and
> there rooted betwixt them such an affection, which
> cannot choose but branch now. Since their more ma-
> ture dignities and royal necessaries make separation
> of their society, their encounters, though not per-
> sonal, have been royally attorneyed, with interchange
> of gifts, letters, loving embassies . . . (1.1.18–24)

The oneness of childhood gives way to the "branchedness" of
adulthood. The innocent boy becomes a competitive man, and
competitiveness is what ultimately poisons Leontes against his
friend and his wife. When he first asks Polixenes to prolong his
visit in Sicilia, he is refused. But when he instructs his wife to
try her hand at persuasion, she succeeds: Polixenes agrees to

stay. This seems to be the trigger to Leontes' jealousy, helped by his recollection of how difficult it was for him to win his wife's hand in marriage years before:

> Three crabbed months had soured themselves to death,
> Ere I could make thee open thy white hand
> And clap thyself my love. (1.2.102–104)

Competitiveness and difficulty seem to be at issue here, not just sexual jealousy—or rather, sexual jealousy as the byproduct of a "fall" from oneness and ease into competitiveness and difficulty.

Jealousy bred out of competition is a toxic agent that deforms Leontes' relationships to those he loves. No one in his circle can believe that Hermione was unfaithful. And yet the circumstances in which he has grown up and married, which we can understand if we attend closely to the lines of the play, help account for his seemingly irrational behavior. As with Othello, whose jealousy seems paranoid and irrational from the outside but which springs from inner doubts and fears that Iago is able to exploit, Leontes is presented to us as conditioned to a similar jealousy as a result of his inability to cope with the pressures of adulthood.

If the first half of the play is *Hamlet*-like in its focus on a longing for lost childhood and the kind of mental anguish and irrational action that such longing can elicit, the second half is *Lear*-like in dealing with parenting and the different competitive issues relating to separation that it elicits. In act 3, we switch from Sicilia to Bohemia (Polixenes' kingdom), where Leontes' infant daughter has been left to die in the wilderness. (The coincidence is explained by a dream that directs Leontes' emissary, Paulina's husband, Antigonus, to name the baby Perdita and abandon her in that country.) But instead of perishing, Perdita is found and raised by simple shepherds.

In act 4, we are informed that sixteen years have passed and Perdita has grown into a beautiful woman. In proper fairy-tale fashion, Polixenes' son, Florizel, has happened upon her in the course of his wanderings through the forest and fallen in love with and engaged himself to her. When Polixenes learns what Florizel is up to, he visits the shepherd's cottage in disguise.

In a scene that parallels Leontes' jealous eruption in act 1, Polixenes erupts in rage when Florizel, not knowing to whom he is speaking, admits that he has not told his father about his engagement. Like Lear, Polixenes feels betrayed by a much-loved child. Lear expected his daughter to express her devotion to him in a certain way; Polixenes expects his son to confide in him and follow a prescribed course in choosing a wife. In both cases, a child's not doing what is expected is seen by the father as a repudiation of his authority.

The separation of the prince from his father is a replication of the separation of Leontes from Polixenes when they left boyhood behind. Child-child bonds and parent-child bonds are similar in that they entail a period of mutual dependence that leads inevitably to a separation, and to a sense of loss that can spur competition and jealousy.

The anatomization of these feelings seems to me so simple and powerful that, though the characters are not extensively developed and behave in reprehensible ways, they are nonetheless deeply empathetic. The play makes Leontes look irrational in his suspicion (everyone around him is adamant in denying that his wife has been unfaithful), but if we insert ourselves into his point of view we can understand what aroused it: Hermione's flirtatious manner, Polixenes' acquiescence to her plea that he stay on after having refused his friend, and the coincidence of the nine-month visit with the end of her pregnancy. Although my students are slow to understand Leontes' outburst, I know that others of my age and experience have seen some basis for his suspicion of his wife and friend.

Similarly, in the case of Polixenes, most parents (of whom I am one) empathize with his outrage, while most students, not being parents, do not. I should note that the same kind of parental response occurs in *Othello* when Brabantio, Desdemona's father, learns that his daughter has willingly married, without his knowledge, a man he had never envisioned as a son-in-law:

> I am glad at soul I have no other child,
> For thy escape would teach me tyranny
> To hang clogs on them. (1.3.194–196)

I have taught *Othello* to older African American women, all of them parents, who despite their acute sensitivity to the racism in the play, still say they empathize with Brabantio's outrage at having his child act behind his back. Florizel, like Desdemona, has been secretive in his actions and acknowledges that he has no intention of informing his father of his plans to marry.

His choice of a shepherdess over a princess also raises the issue of class, present but eclipsed by the issue of race in *Othello*. Shakespeare makes class prejudice central to *The Winter's Tale* and addresses it metaphorically in a wonderful passage in which Polixenes, still in disguise, lectures Perdita about the "natural" art of grafting flowers:

> You see, sweet maid, we marry
> A gentler scion of the wildest stock,
> And make conceive a bark of baser kind
> By bud of nobler race. This is an art
> Which does mend nature—change it rather—but
> The art itself is nature. (4.4.92–97)

This is a simple and elegant argument on behalf of intermarriage—
a lovely refutation of Iago's assertion that Othello's marriage to
Desdemona is "unnatural." Ironically, it is Polixenes, the man who
opposes his son's marriage to a shepherdess, who speaks these
lines, while it is Perdita, who plans to marry above her apparent
station, who disagrees:

> I'll not put
> The dibble in the earth, to set one slip of them;
> No more than, were I painted, I would wish
> This youth should say 'twere well, and only therefore
> Desire to breed with me. (4.4.99–103)

Given who speaks which lines in this argument, Shakespeare
seems to want to demonstrate how hard it is to practice what
we preach—to transfer what we can accept in an abstract situation to what we can accept in an analogous one that pertains
directly and viscerally to us. This was the lesson of *Measure for
Measure*. It also reminds us that we may understand an idea in
one context and fail to see its applicability in another. Perdita
can understand the cross-breeding of flowers as a metaphor for
wearing makeup and decry it as something she would never
do. But she fails to make the more obvious connection to intermarriage, in which she is prepared to engage. Students will
protest that intermarriage is more "natural" than makeup, but
this leads into a repetition of the debate as to what is natural in
human society and what is artificial.

Some students argue that Perdita's lower-class status cannot
be taken seriously since it is an illusion. Shakespeare has stacked
the deck so that the seeming shepherdess is, in fact, a princess,
supporting class prejudice under the cover of critiquing it. Others argue that Perdita, raised from infancy in a rustic setting,
effectively belongs to the class in which she was raised. This

leads into the age-old nature versus nurture debate that crops up so often in Shakespeare and that can never be fully resolved.

The final and most debated scene of the play occurs when the characters assemble back in the court of Sicilia after a long series of circuitous and farcical events. Perdita's identity has been revealed, and everyone present is reconciled to everyone else. Paulina now leads the group to view a statue of the assumed-dead Hermione—a wonderful likeness in which the figure has been aged so that she looks as she would have in the present. After all have wondered at this work of art for an appropriate length of time, Paulina instructs the assemblage:

> It is required
> You do awake your faith. Then all stand still.
> On! Those that think it is unlawful business
> I am about, let them depart. (5.3.94–97)

Then: "Music, awake her: strike, / 'Tis time; descend; be stone no more." As Paulina continues her invocation, the statue "stirs" and comes down from its pedestal. Hermione, alive again, is now back in the family circle, able to take her place as Leontes' wife and Perdita's mother. All rejoice, and Leontes bids Paulina,

> Lead us from hence, where we may leisurely
> Each one demand and answer to his part
> Performed in this wide gap of time since first
> We were dissevered. Hastily lead away. (5.3.152–155)

This ending leaves us to puzzle over how Hermione's resurrection will be explained in the ensuing "demand and answer." We must fill it in for ourselves.

Some critics see the final scene as a cheap trick, others as a marvelous piece of stagecraft. I tend to think that the death and resurrection, whether understood as real or contrived, is what Shakespeare saw as the only way possible for Leontes to achieve forgiveness for his behavior in the first act. How does one excuse the inexcusable? Even if Hermione were guilty, it would not justify Leontes' treatment of her, which caused the trauma that killed their young son and sent an innocent baby away to die. There is no coming back from that kind of behavior except through agonizing penance and an act of apparent magic.

But there is another way to look at the ending. We tend to think about the play from Leontes' point of view. He is the jealous tyrant who must be punished and forgiven. But my female students have in recent years been inclined to read it from Hermione and Paulina's perspective, women positioned in the background but nonetheless possessed of an emotional charge that electrifies the play. Both are presented as strong personalities, unwilling to be manipulated or destroyed by patriarchal caprice. One argument goes that Hermione and Paulina have been living peacefully together, whether romantically or in profound friendship, for sixteen years. With the return of Perdita, Hermione can return to the world and to her husband, who has been changed in the course of time by living under the rule of Paulina.

The shifting of male and female authority in this play (from Leontes to Paulina), the awareness of the problematics of class prejudice, the keen sense of how we experience loss in growing up and later in parenting adult children, and the way in which competitiveness structures our lives, even with those we most love—all these themes have been central to Shakespeare's greatest plays and are presented here with a simplicity and clarity that has never been equaled. When Leontes bids Paulina marry Camillo, loyal counselor to both Leontes and Polixenes, in his last speech, this may seem to echo the Duke's proposal to Isabella at the end of *Measure for Measure,* but in fact it reads more like a plea than an edict. Its main function, I believe, is to remind us that all has not been repaired. The final festivities are shadowed by the deaths sixteen years earlier of Leontes and Hermione's young son, Mamillius, and of Paulina's husband, Antigonus (whose fate, after he abandons the baby Perdita in the wilds of Bohemia, is encapsulated in Shakespeare's most famous stage direction: "Exit pursued by a bear"). These are irretrievable losses for which no one can fully compensate.[1] They remind us that life oscillates between the tragic and the festive—that while we can find joy at intervals, we should cherish them as wonderful moments, magical and fleeting. But we are also sentenced to death, like all who came before us. We must feel for our fellow men and women as well as ourselves as we struggle to be happy in the midst of guilt, frailty, and loss.

Conclusion

When multiculturalism began to gain traction in the university three decades ago, it took aim at Shakespeare with particular force. He was labeled the quintessential dead white European male: sexist, racist, and anti-Semitic. While the antagonism has subsided since the deconstructionist fervor of the 1980s, Shakespeare is still taken to task for being complicit in the exploitative, imperialistic nature of his society.

The case against him turns on many factors, but most notable among them is that a Jew is the villain in *The Merchant of Venice*, a black man kills his white wife in *Othello*, and female characters, even when they assert themselves, are returned to conventional heterosexual roles and succumb to patriarchal authority in the end.

In the previous pages I have argued that Shakespeare became increasingly aware of the prejudice and exploitation of his society, and that his plays are primers to awareness and empathy in us.

I would maintain that the negative assumptions that dog the study of Shakespeare have to do in large part with the production history of his plays. Since he wrote them to be performed, this makes sense; yet performance has often served as a handicap to appreciating his empathetic imagination.

Take, for example, the case of Shylock. Before the nineteenth century, this character was represented in the red wig and black cloak associated with the devil in a medieval morality play. Even in the nineteenth century, when a more sympathetic view was popularized by the actors Edmund Kean and Henry Irving, the character was portrayed as profoundly alien and atavistic, moving furtively among more recognizable modern characters. This alien "look" was capitalized on in the twentieth century when *The Merchant of Venice* became a favorite of the Third Reich, and a hunched and hook-nosed Shylock became a trope for the villainous, subhuman Jew in Nazi propaganda.

But Shakespeare makes a point of contradicting the idea that Shylock is physically distinct in the way that most productions, even up through the present, have portrayed him. While it is true that the character asserts his difference from the Christian characters, it is also true that he is not necessarily dramatically Other in appearance. When Portia, in disguise as the young male lawyer Balthazar, enters the courtroom, she asks: "Which is the merchant here? And which the Jew?" I have seen these questions played for laughs—as though the difference is patently obvious—but there is no indication in the text that the line is meant to be funny. In the same vein, students often assume that the "merchant" in the title of the play is Shylock, not Antonio. And though teachers often respond condescendingly to this confusion, I think Shakespeare may have intended it. Both Antonio and Shylock are involved with commerce; both are marginal characters with respect to the main and mainstream characters; and both are loose ends at the conclusion of the play. Portia's question is important because it suggests that they could be mistaken for each other and are mutually dependent in many ways.

Understanding the symbiosis of these two characters strikes me as historically insightful—and honest about how bigotry works to create villains like Shylock. Indeed, I prefer the play's hard truth to unrealistically philo-Semitic treatments by George Eliot, for example, in *Daniel Deronda,* where the Jewish characters are heavily idealized, and by Charles Dickens in *Our Mutual Friend,* where the preternaturally gentle Riah seems designed to correct for his anti-Semitic rendering of Fagin in *Oliver Twist.*

The outline of *The Merchant of Venice,* comic in its general thrust but incorporating the harrowing scene in which Shylock is shamed, stripped of his fortune, and forced to convert, has caused some of the most enthusiastic Shakespeare scholars to label it anti-Semitic. Yet to me, this is a dramatic form of disruption, a way of making viewers and readers think more deeply and feelingly about the dubious nature of justice, and how the suffering of others whom we fail to see may lurk behind a seemingly happy ending.

Othello has been similarly affected by its production history. Up through the middle of the twentieth century, white men performed the title role in blackface.[1] This casting implicitly supported Iago's argument that it was "unnatural" for a black man to have courted and married Desdemona. "It would be something monstrous to conceive this beautiful Venetian girl falling in love with a veritable Negro," pronounced the Romantic poet and critic Samuel Taylor Coleridge. Although the Romantics allied themselves with the outsider position, they did so only, apparently, when the outsider shared their skin color. By casting a white man in the role of Othello, the "monstrous" effect that Coleridge feared could be eliminated; blackness could be made into a costume element rather than an essential part of the plot. Hence, for many years—including when I read the play in high school—teachers made no mention of race, focusing instead on the destructive effects of jealousy, as though it had sprung up without any context. White men in black makeup (or brown, since in some productions Othello was conceived to be an Arab rather than an African) continued to be cast in the role up through the mid-twentieth century.[2]

These stagings of Shakespeare, profoundly offensive to us now, reflect the limited perspective of when and where they were produced. No era is immune from such limitation. When we see contemporary productions that seem relevant and enlightened, we ought to suspect that they harbor biases that are invisible to us. I still await a production of *Othello,* for example, that represents Iago less as an uninflected villain and more as the victim of class prejudice.[3]

"We're *in* society, aren't we, and that's our horizon?" comments a character in a Henry James novel.[4] The question expresses resignation on the part of the character and, I think, of James himself to the limitations imposed by a given positioning in time and place. As much as I admire Henry James as a master of subtlety and intelligence in many respects, I wince at the way he depicts Jewish characters in his last novel, *The Golden Bowl,* and the way he describes Jews on the Lower East Side of Manhattan in his memoir, *The American Scene.* James was deeply attuned to the cruelty that can lie behind refined social discourse, but he was, nonetheless, a participant in some of the cruelest prejudices of his age.

But Shakespeare was different. He was, through unusual sensitivity and continual practice, able to see beyond his society's horizon. He does not idealize either Shylock or Othello or, for that matter, Antonio or Portia, Hamlet or Lear. But he empathizes with them and makes it possible for us to understand their point of view. He alerts us to the fact that we may be blind to our own motives, fears, and desires. Indeed, I know that my reading of Shakespeare in this book is conditioned by societal constraints and by the indelible facts that make up my individual being. But this awareness is also a spur to revision and change. Taking Shakespeare's evolution as a guide, I can try to stretch beyond my society's horizon and to extend my capacity for empathy into new arenas. This is always the goal as I read and teach the plays.

The accusations of racism, sexism, and anti-Semitism leveled against Shakespeare are often a way of indicting the past for being racist, sexist, and anti-Semitic and, in doing so, of feeling superior to it. This strikes me as both historically unempathetic and critically lazy. There is no doubt that Shakespeare was describing the society in which he lived, one that was predominantly white, Protestant, and patriarchal. But this was the norm against which deviations occurred—not least the presence on the throne of a powerful female monarch—and within which Otherness lived and suffered out of sight of mainstream ideas and values. Shakespeare, without being a propagandist or a revolutionary, made deviation and Otherness central to the drama and interest of his plays. Yet to see this requires a certain kind of sustained attention.

Which brings me back to the point made in my Introduction about the value of *reading* Shakespeare. To read the plays is to see things that directors, functioning within the constraints of a singular production, may miss or choose to ignore. To be fair, a production *has* to be a singular interpretation. To include too much would make the play impossible to follow within the time involved in its staging.

The value of close reading, however, is that it need not be confined to a few hours. It can be drawn out over the course of days or even weeks. (I once taught a course on *King Lear* that extended over a ten-week term.) Close reading allows multiple interpretations, often at cross-purposes to one another, to exist simultaneously. "Do I contradict myself? Very well, I contradict myself," wrote Walt Whitman, the great American poet, who might have been a character out of Shakespeare in his vivid expressiveness—a Falstaff with a commitment to social justice. Reading Shakespeare in a classroom, and especially around a seminar table at which every opinion can be challenged, is a special kind of intellectual adventure—a spur to open-mindedness and empathy.

Shakespeare had the ability to learn from past patterns of thought and move farther and farther away from the conventional thinking and prejudices of his time—to embrace a more empathetic view of humanity, no matter how peripheral his subjects were to his own experience. This gift, unique in my opinion in the history of literature, makes it crucial that we place Shakespeare at the center of the academic curriculum—that we insist that our children read him, not just go to productions or movies that adapt the plays to the views of the moment, however ecumenical that moment may seem to us. If we can read, discuss, and debate the complex meanings that underlie Shakespeare's plays in the context of the historical factors that defined his world, we will come some way toward being able to do the same with our own.

Notes

Introduction

1. Harold Bloom (1930–2019) was a towering figure in literary criticism and a self-anointed authority on Shakespeare's genius. In the last decade of his life, he focused on Shakespearean "personalities," with individual books on Falstaff, Cleopatra, and Lear. Bloom was also a great advocate for reading Shakespeare and boasted that he preferred imagining the plays to seeing them performed.

2. My use of *empathy* reflects principally what Stephanie D. Preston and Alicia J. Hofelich define as "True Empathy: A compassionate, other-oriented state that requires a distinction in the observer between self and other" ("The Many Faces of Empathy," *Emotion Review* 20, no. 10 [2011]: 1–10). My discussion of *Hamlet,* however, also conforms to what they refer to as "Self-Other Overlap: Correspondence between observer and target."

1
Shakespeare's Empathetic Imagination

1. The Great Chain of Being had its origins in classical philosophy. Both Plato and Aristotle provide the foundation taken up by medieval Scholastics and passed on to the great sixteenth- and seventeenth-century writers, Shakespeare being the most notable. The concept was first brought to the attention of scholars by Arthur O. Lovejoy in *The Great Chain of Being: A Study of the History of an Idea* (Cambridge: Harvard University Press, 1936) and further developed by E. M. W. Tillyard in *The Elizabethan World Picture: A Study of the Idea of Order in the Age of Shakespeare, Donne, and Milton* (London:

Chatto and Windus, 1943). When I was an undergraduate majoring in English in the 1970s, these books were widely referenced. I do not think that the Great Chain of Being has ever been refuted as influential in the thinking of Shakespeare. Indeed, the model can be seen to underlie and support white patriarchal oppression in Western culture. Nonetheless, as Shakespeare used it in his empathetic rendering of character, it also paved the way for its critique and dismantling by students of multiculturalism.

2. To understand this statement, consider how William James, the great philosopher turned father of American psychology, defined the role of *habit*—which is to say, behavioral structure—in the formation of character: "When we look at living creatures from an outward point of view, one of the first things that strike us is that they are bundles of habits" (*The Principles of Psychology* [New York: Henry Holt, 1890], 104). From this premise, James proposed a conception of emotion based on habit: "By regulating the action, which is under the more direct control of the will, we can indirectly regulate the feeling" ("The Gospel of Relaxation," *Scribner's Magazine* 25 [1899]: 500. Elsewhere, he presents this idea as a reversal of expected cause and effect in the realm of emotion: we do not cry because we are sad, we are sad because we cry.

3. There has been voluminous speculation on Shakespeare's life, but very few facts have been found that can be relied on as unequivocally true. A comprehensive and historically informed biography of the playwright is Stephen Greenblatt's *Will in the World: How Shakespeare Became Shakespeare* (New York: Norton, 2004). Greenblatt has spent a lifetime steeped in the historical context of Elizabethan England. Yet his book, full of facts about the period though it is, remains speculative. My argument that Shakespeare learned empathy over the course of his writing career is similarly speculative but informed by two decades of teaching undergraduate students and, perhaps most important, my struggles as a novelist. Much the way second-rate baseball players can become good coaches because of how hard they had to work to achieve competence, I see my middling abilities as a fiction writer as giving me unique insight into Shakespeare's creative process.

4. McLuhan begins his most famous book, *Understanding Media: The Extensions of Man* (New York: McGraw Hill, 1964), with this statement: "In a culture like ours, long accustomed to splitting and dividing all things as a means of control, it is sometimes a bit of a shock to be reminded that, in operational and practical fact, the medium is the message. This is merely to say that the personal and social consequences of any medium—that is, of any extension of ourselves—result from the new scale that is introduced into our affairs by each extension of ourselves, or by any new technology" (7). The key notion of relevance to Shakespeare is that the medium—the form—is an "extension of ourselves." Shakespeare's plays express, formally, who he was within his particular culture. But he and his form together helped shape the human being he became and who lives on in our cultural pantheon.

2
Richard III

1. Unlike Gloucester, Caliban can also be seen as explicitly the product of bad parenting, whether we blame his mother, the witch Sycorax, as Prospero does, or his foster father, Prospero himself, as postcolonialist critics of the play do. See Stephen Greenblatt's *Learning to Curse: Essays in Early Modern Culture* (New York: Routledge, 1992) for the landmark postcolonial approach to Caliban.

3
Richard II, Henry IV, and *Henry V*

1. Arthur Pittis, an educator and dramaturge, suggested to me that Shakespeare must have learned a great deal from watching the actors in his troupe play multiple roles and hearing them discuss these roles as they informed their acting choices. This may have been a spur to greater depth and empathy in his creation of subsequent characters.

4
The Merchant of Venice

1. Heither Heim, a Drexel University English major who checked my citations in this book, made the astute observation that Shakespeare's promiscuous borrowing from other sources may be better understood now in light of contemporary open-access arguments with regard to the internet. Indeed, I believe that we may be on the verge of returning to a more fluid concept of creativity which, though obviously different, has elements in common with what existed in Shakespeare's time.

5
As You Like It

1. Marjorie Garber in *Vested Interests: Cross-Dressing and Cultural Anxiety* (New York: Penguin, 1993) grounds her insights into cross-dressing as a cultural phenomenon in her study of Shakespeare.

6
Hamlet

1. The issue of succession in *Hamlet* has been raised in the Shakespeare literature. It seems that Denmark was an electoral monarchy (a group of Electors determined the next king) and that Shakespeare may have been aware of this when he has Claudius worry about the popularity of Hamlet and Laertes. But I tend to think that we do not want to take this historical fact too far. I agree with the venerable mid-twentieth-century Shakespeare critic J. Dover Wilson, who argued that Denmark was a stand-in for England, that Claudius was a usurper, and that Hamlet was meant to be the legitimate heir; see his *What Happens in Hamlet* (Cambridge: Cambridge University Press, 1962). I believe Shakespeare wanted us to recognize this while also relaying the fact that Hamlet's attention was focused elsewhere.

7
Othello

1. I suppose the most cogent example I can think of is our failure to "see" animal suffering. Isaac Bashevis Singer put this eloquently: "For the animals it is an eternal Treblinka" ("The Letter Writer," in Singer, *The Collected Stories* [New York: Farrar Straus and Giroux, 1982], 271).

2. That Othello's blackness allows an easier indictment of prejudice in dramatizing the superficial nature of exclusion based on skin color will not work if the viewer cannot visually register the point. This is demonstrated by the ingrained prejudices that for so long kept black actors from the role. Indeed, blackness has often served as a foil for whiteness, allowing some to assimilate at the expense of others. For example, in the 1927 pioneering sound film *The Jazz Singer,* blackface becomes a means of assimilation for the Jewish protagonist; when he takes off his blackface makeup, he becomes more white and less Jewish through the contrast.

8
King Lear

1. Critics have placed a great deal of emphasis on the moment when Lear urges the Fool to seek shelter from the storm ahead of himself: "In, boy, go first. You houseless poverty— / Nay, get thee in; I'll pray, and then I'll sleep" (3.4.26–27). Giving precedence to another, weaker individual does reflect a change in Lear's behavior. The Fool also disappears from the play after these

words, making them seem all the more significant. But if Lear assumes an empathetic paternal role in this passage, it must be noted that the Fool is not actually his child and has no leverage over him, as Cordelia does.

9
Measure for Measure

1. The most frequently cited "problem plays" are *All's Well That Ends Well, Measure for Measure,* and *Troilus and Cressida,* to which are often added *The Merchant of Venice, Antony and Cleopatra,* and *The Winter's Tale.*

2. The bed trick could be traced back to the Old Testament substitution of Leah for Rachel on Jacob's wedding night. It is exhaustively discussed as a literary and cultural motif in Wendy Doniger's *The Bedtrick: Tales of Sex and Masquerade* (Chicago: University of Chicago Press, 2000).

3. The production was in April 2019 at the Lantern Theater in Philadelphia.

10
Antony and Cleopatra

1. I am using the term "ally" as it is sometimes used in explicating the last letter in the acronym: LGBTQA (lesbian, gay, bisexual, transgender, queer, ally—though A has also been understood to refer to "asexual").

11
The Winter's Tale

1. Some of my students are bothered that the only mention of Mamillius in the last act comes when Leontes is fleetingly reminded of him when he sees Florizel ("Had our prince, / Jewel of children, seen this hour, he had paired / Well with this lord" [5.1.115–117]). But more attention to that loss would dim the celebration. I am reminded of the lesson the director Alfred Hitchcock learned after releasing his 1936 film, *Sabotage* (based on Joseph Conrad's novel *The Secret Agent*), which included the death of the heroine's young brother. "It was a grave error on my part," Hitchcock said, to explain the movie's poor box office (François Truffaut, *Hitchcock* [New York: Simon and Schuster, 1983], 109).

Conclusion

1. Ira Aldridge, an African American actor, performed throughout Europe and Russia in the role (and in white face as other Shakespearean characters) in the nineteenth century, though thwarted from performing in America. The great black actor and activist Paul Robeson performed the role in London in 1930 and to great acclaim on Broadway in 1942—but not without heckling and severe criticism in some quarters. Despite his success, however, white actors continued to perform the role up until near the end of the twentieth century. The last known film performance of the role by a white actor was in 1981 by Anthony Hopkins.

2. It is interesting to consider that white Christian men played Othello and Shylock in Shakespeare's day. This kind of casting would later become a way to obscure difference and block empathy, but at the time Shakespeare wrote, Jews and black people were in short supply in British society. The effect would have been to inspire empathy for these marginal characters, much in the way men playing women (itself the result of societal prejudice), in Shakespeare's hands, inspired empathy for the female position.

3. The 1981 film version of the play starred Bob Hoskins as Iago with a cockney accent but ironically cast Anthony Hopkins in blackface as Othello (probably the last such instance of this). A 2013 Royal Shakespeare production also gave Iago a cockney accent, but failed to fully delineate the class difference by giving his wife Emilia the same refined accent as the other characters.

4. The statement is made by Mr. Longdon, a Jamesian surrogate, in James's late novel *The Awkward Age* (New York: Harper's, 1899), 165.

Index

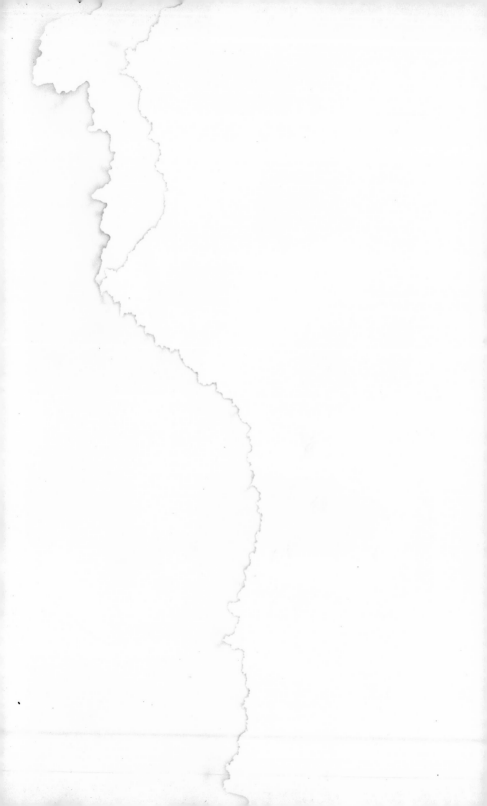